Celebrating Jesus Christ
in Africa

FAITH AND CULTURES SERIES

An Orbis Series on Contextualizing Gospel and Church
General Editor: Robert J. Schreiter, C.PP.S.

The *Faith and Cultures Series* deals with questions that arise as Christian faith attempts to respond to its new global reality. For centuries Christianity and the church were identified with European cultures. Although the roots of Christian tradition lie deep in Semitic cultures and Africa, and although Asian influences on it are well documented, that original diversity was widely forgotten as the church took shape in the West.

Today, as the churches of the Americas, Asia, and Africa take their place alongside older churches of Mediterranean and North Atlantic cultures, they claim the right to express Christian faith in their own idioms, thought patterns, and cultures. To provide a forum for better understanding this process, the Orbis *Faith and Cultures Series* publishes books that illuminate the range of questions that arise from this global challenge.

Orbis and the *Faith and Cultures Series* General Editor invite the submission of manuscripts on relevant topics.

Also in the Series

FAITH AND CULTURES SERIES

Celebrating Jesus Christ in Africa

Liturgy and Inculturation

François Kabasele Lumbala

ORBIS BOOKS

Maryknoll, New York 10545

The Catholic Foreign Mission Society of America (Maryknoll) recruits and trains people for overseas missionary service. Through Orbis Books, Maryknoll aims to foster the international dialogue that is essential to mission. The books published, however, reflect the opinions of their authors and are not meant to represent the official position of the Society.

Library of Congress Cataloging in Publication Data

Kabasele Lumbala, François.
     Celebrating Jesus Christ in Africa : liturgy and inculturation /
François Kabasele Lumbala.
          p.   cm.   —   (Faith and cultures series)
     Includes bibliographical references.
     ISBN 0-88344-971-4 (pbk.)
     Catholic Church—Africa, Sub-Saharan—Liturgy—Texts—History
and criticism.   2. Christianity and culture—Africa, Sub-Saharan.
3. Catholic Church—Liturgy, Experimental.   4. Liturgical
adaptation.   I. Title.   II. Series.
BX1977.A357K33   1998
264'.02'00967—dc21   98-16478
                                                           CIP

Contents

Foreword

David N. Power, O.M.I.

The principles of liturgical adaptation enunciated at the Second Vatican Council are well known. They have provoked many studies on the concepts of adaptation, accommodation, inculturation, incarnation, and contextualization, as these apply to the spread of the gospel and to the liturgy. In historical studies, some attention has been given to how cultural influences played a role in times past, for example, in the eight-century adaptation of the Roman rite to Frankish peoples. In considering the relation between liturgy and culture as a current issue, most often it is studied in terms of liturgical expression in non-Western churches. Though the concern also affects older churches, in Africa or Asia it seems clearer that revising liturgies is no simple matter of incorporating some ritual actions or images into the Roman liturgy; in the long run the question is whether the Roman tradition or the new local rites or liturgical families are in the process of emerging as new cultural creations.

However many the theoretical discussions of liturgy and culture, it is in the *practice* of worship that one sees what is involved and from it that insight is gained into the process and its norms. Innovations found serviceable in any church provide models for other churches as they endeavor to assess their own developments. For this reason the study presented in these pages by Kabasele is of value not only in informing readers about worship in the churches of Africa, but in offering wisdom to other churches facing questions about possible developments in their own liturgies.

The process of integrating liturgical traditions and cultural traditions is not predetermined by an application of general principles. To assess adequately its practical evolution, three attitudes are indispensable: openness to all that is other to one's own tradition; critical judgment on the extent to which historical forms of Christian worship have respected what is authentically human; and genuine spiritual values and channels of commerce with the holy. Kabasele, in his evaluation of African developments, exhibits these qualities of discernment.

Inevitably my reading of his text is done from the vantage point of the Northern hemisphere and cannot be an African reading. It is offered here simply as a way of expressing what might be learned by way of more general liturgical principles by reflection on what is occurring in Africa.

LITURGY AND AFRICAN CULTURE

Kabasele offers examples of recent liturgical development in several African churches, not confining himself to his own Church of Zaire. His work provides fascinating reading as one sees how patterns of rite and prayer emerge in such services as the eucharistic action, the celebration of the other sacraments, blessings, religious profession, and funeral rites. The variety of examples compels the reader to avoid the easy solution of simply "thinking African" and to recognize the plurality within Africa itself.

Some matters are, of course, general to African cultural developments and provide food for thought to other peoples. For one thing, African cultures are impregnated with the sense of the religious and the holy, so that in Africa attention to culture and the encounter of the Christian religion with other religions go together. For peoples who like to separate their religion and their common cultural values, this is a reminder that, however legitimate or necessary the distinction, it is not possible to banish the question of the transcendent and of communion with the spiritual world, however this is conceived, from any sphere of life. For the inculturation of the liturgy on all continents, this is a reminder that the incorporation of any cultural pattern must face the question of how well its symbolically expressed values harmonize with the gospel.

THE HOLY OF THE OTHER

There is a great openness in Kabasele's work to the meaning and truth of traditional religions and to the presence of the religious in all aspects of traditional cultures. Rather than risking a curtailment of the gospel or a disregard for historical forms of worship, this actually results in a new appreciation of the gospel and of the history and rites of Christian worship. It brings out what living the gospel means in terms of a respect for the human person and human community, and in terms of its potential to affirm and integrate aspects of the human that are best expressed in the symbols, rites, and practices of traditional cultures and religions. Integral to this are the senses of human wholeness and spiritual vitality that pervade all of human life and put it in touch with greater spiritual forces, or with the pervasively holy. Instead of being suspicious of this attitude or globally classifying it with derogatory religious terms, such as superstition or polytheism or animism, Christian churches may learn from it what is lacking in their own religious sensitivity. The gospel loses nothing and gains much in this encounter and in this acknowledgment of the "other."

IN HARMONY WITH THE UNIVERSE

By reason of their spiritual vitality, the African cultural forms described in this work display an innate sense of the harmony of the universe. They are an example of the need for human societies to respect this harmony, and indeed to see themselves as integral to it. African peoples' sense of ritual allows them to give forceful expression to this consonance, and this is carried over into Christian liturgy. Rural Africa and urban Africa, however, have begun to show a differentiation that is evident in other countries also. In the process of the urbanization and the reception of values from other continents that is taking place, one sees the problems that emerge when this sense of harmony fades or when its ritual expression seems more folkloric than real. Hence the question arises as to how something traditional can find expression in new circumstances, not hindering good developments in patterns of living but acting as a critical force in human life.

REMEMBERING ANCESTORS: A LIVING PAST

The sense of harmony affects not only the world of the living present but stretches back to past ages and to the living dead. As Kabasele shows, in the respect given to ancestors and in the rituals or prayers that honor them, there is a sublime awareness of how the present generation lives in vital continuity with the past and of what it owes the past, as well as the risks involved in breaking with the past. The spirits of the ancestors are not only living beings with whom one must even now have commerce, but they represent the value and force of traditions and the ways in which the energies, achievements and sorrows of past history are integral to present and future directions. So particular and important is this communion with ancestors and all that they represent that it is impossible to reduce this cult to the cult of the saints or to the recognition of the place of Old Testament personages in the plan of salvation.

While the cult of the saints in Christian worship respects the communion between the living and dead, it does not equal the African veneration of ancestors in incorporating the dynamism that comes from a respectful communion with past ages and all that their memory represents for the present. On the other hand, the origins of the cult of the saints in the cult of martyrs is a reminder that all Christian memory is enveloped in the memory of Christ's suffering. The early saints were venerated because in their suffering they gave witness to the reality and to the triumph of

Christ's suffering. What edge will it put on the memory of ancestors to see their power in the light of Christ's suffering? Will the memory of Christ's Passover invite African churches to reflect anew on what their people see as worthy of power and respect? Will they perhaps be prompted to include some yet unnamed persons from their past among those worthy of respect and veneration?

BODILY HOLINESS

In the West we tend to associate African worship and the adaptation of Christian worship to African culture with dance and with song. The sense of being in harmony with life's rhythm is expressed in the body. This adds three dimensions to the worship of God. First, revering God requires that the human person have a sense of personal wholeness, without any division in the self between the spirit and the body. Second, it requires respect for the human need to act in accord with the rhythms of nature. Third, it requires harmony and oneness within the community, something that is expressed in the coordinated movements of the dance, danced together rather than alone. The introduction of the dance in some Western churches, as Kabasele remarks, tends to be a solo or a troupe dance, which aids the congregation in its meditation on the scriptures or on the rituals of liturgy. In African liturgies, without any suppression of individuals or of diverse roles, it is the entire body of people that is caught up in the dance. Thus the congregation gives vivid expression to the holiness of harmony within the community and of the community with life's rhythms.

WORSHIP AND SOCIAL HARMONY

Among the other things expressed in bodily ritual is an apprehension of that corporate wholeness that is vital to the movement of social reality. This pervades many other aspects of African ritual, as Kabasele shows in his discussion of the rites of marriage, reconciliation, and mourning. In the name of Christ and the power of the Spirit, liturgy needs to enable people to live their relation to kin, people, and society without causing disruption, either personal or social. This is of great concern in traditional African rites and religions. This is also, however, a domain where the cutting edge of Christian faith and perception can be quite acute. In the quest for patterns, traditional rites risk subjugating the importance and freedom of the individual person. In pursuing what appears to be the common interest, they can also promote a morality called into question by the gospel. Here the church has to both show respect for established social patterns and give testimony to Christ's freedom. A good example from this work is that of the procedure of a widow's mourning ritual. Much of the traditional pattern is kept in what Kabasele describes, but in the end the woman is freed of the traditional obligation of sexual union with the dead husband's brother. In another example, while the patterns of reconciliation demonstrate how sin and pardon affect the social body, the Christian edge given to these rites expresses a deeper concern with the heart and the life of the individual sinner.

IMAGINATION AND LANGUAGE

The final area of concern here is that of the creativity of linguistic expression. All peoples must worship God and remember Christ from within their own imaginative and language patterns. Since so much Christian teaching and ritual is set in patterns that have developed in countries of the North, and has been set for some time in its essentials, there is an authoritative tendency to translate rather than create new acclamations, songs, and prayers. Greater or lesser flexibility is shown in this translation, as the case may be, and some new prayers are allowed that are assessed on the basis of traditional images and forms of address. Looking to other continents, some writers speak of "dynamic equivalence." By this they mean, in short, that traditional beliefs, perceptions, and prayers can be rewritten to allow for more affective expression and a greater imaginative appeal that evokes the experience and the traditional prayers of other peoples.

However, once placed within a language other than one's own, one realizes that this evolves quite a different view of the world and of life. God and Christ have then to be "thought," as it were, and given a name and an address from within this other language. Some of the African prayers mentioned in this work bear serious reflection in terms of understanding the patterns of language expression, as well as the creative freedom, that traditional Christian forms can allow.

One example in Kabasele's study is particularly striking, in view of the innumerable studies that have been devoted of late to the history of the eucharistic prayer and its different forms. Though some argument continues as to its common and essential pattern, new books of worship in Anglican, Catholic, or Lutheran churches set down the normative pattern and the essential parts of the prayer. When one looks at African prayers, one cannot but help notice not only their imagery but an emergence of new forms that nonetheless retain a continuity with the Christian past. Remembering Christ within African linguistic patterns and then addressing God in virtue of this memory erupts in forms of prayer that do not simply reflect Semitic or Greco-Roman mentalities and ways of expression. When one then goes back from this newness to the history and traditional variety of the prayer, one comes away with a fresh discovery of its adaptability and innovative potential. There is no more dynamic equivalence at work in this, but fresh theological horizons are opened up.

CONCLUSION

Whenever there is a genuine and generous recognition of the existence, truth, and authenticity of the other, there is an expansion of one's own consciousness and of faith's possibilities. Western churches have by no means been ultra-successful in allowing the remembrance of Christ to find cultural resonance in their own acts of worship. In letting themselves be faced with the other in African churches and African culture, they may be spurred to a more imaginative approach to their own development of appropriate forms of liturgy. Apart from what it does to foster communion between churches, we may be grateful to Kabasele for providing us with the information and the wisdom that calls us to a genuine colloquy with the other of African liturgy.

Introduction

In the subsequent chapters, examples of a variety of African ritual celebrations of the salvation through Jesus Christ are described. These rites are not fully approved as yet by Roman law regulating divine worship, nor are they universally practiced throughout Africa. Nonetheless, they enjoy a modified tolerance, a tolerance sometimes held suspect by the local ecclesiastical hierarchy and given a provisional approbation and limited geographically to certain dioceses and parishes in Africa. This conforms with the *Constitution on the Sacred Liturgy*, which stipulates:

> So that adaptation is made with the necessary circumspection, faculties will be given by the Apostolic See to the territorial ecclesiastical authority to permit and direct the necessary preliminary experiences in certain appropriate assemblies for limited times (no. 40, 2).

The Zairian rite of the mass has been in place in communities since 1967. On 30 April 1988 it was approved after multiple versions and diplomatic rewriting of sections of the text. Even the title indicates the level of concern over maintaining unity: *The Roman Missal for the Dioceses of Zaire*.

Africans have not waited for official approbation to try to "speak and confess Jesus Christ," to "celebrate salvation in Jesus" in a way that represents them and in the way in which they perceive it. Official approval has always followed the actual life of the community. But this process does not have to give way to anarchy. One cannot celebrate in a Christian way without communion with the hierarchy of the church. Liturgy by nature is a communal act and therefore submits to an organization. And so different initiatives are submitted to the local hierarchy, who presides prudently over liturgical development.

By portraying these liturgical experiences, I hope to draw the fundamental lines of their evolution in relation to the Christian tradition. This will show the cultural resources that new African symbols bring to Christian inculturation. It seems to me that this type of presentation will reveal the potential restructuring of different symbols.

In the first chapter we deal with rites and human imprint; we begin with this subject because it is one of the principal reasons why the rites are changing in Africa. In the second chapter we look at baptism and confirmation in Africa. In the third we discuss the eucharist, the summit of sacramental structure and the rite with which Christian communities are most frequently confronted, to which they are most often invited. Penance and reconciliation, marriage, anointing of the sick, and ordination are treated in the following chapters. After the sacraments, in another chapter, we discuss briefly blessings and consecrations that relate specifically to the African way of life. The last chapter looks at which church, which society, and which theology are designed in those African rites.

A word on the arrangement of themes is called for. I have written with several goals in mind. First and foremost, writing for the Orbis Faith and Cultures Series, I hope to help my fellow Christians and other students of African religions understand better the actual practice of Christian worship in a range of African cultures. My own experience revolves around French-speaking Africa, chiefly in Congo and Cameroon, and slightly around English-speaking Africa, such as Nigeria, Zambia, and Malawi.

1

The Human Imprint
on the Liturgy

In 1983 I defended a thesis on the rites of religious consecration in Africa. There, much attention was focused upon the rite of the pact of blood, which involved placing a drop of the candidate's blood on an altar cloth. One of the reactions against this African ritual was addressed to me in these terms: "The sight of blood in a Christian ritual is embarrassing, because in Christian liturgy we prefer to use symbols rather than concrete things themselves. When Christ speaks of his blood, he presents a little wine; he doesn't shed his blood." My response was brief: Christ didn't shed his blood in the cup because what he wanted to signify in speaking of blood was his life as "food." It is for this reason that he takes real food (bread and wine). But in the rite of religious profession, what the candidate wants to signify is the definitive character of his or her covenant with Christ: the blood of this human person becomes the matter where the message of the definitive union is formed.

This reaction was primarily because of a particular "current" in Christianity, a current that represses the body—and whatever can be sensed, whatever is related to the flesh—as unfit for the Spirit. Nevertheless, matter is the place where the Spirit is at work, the place where we have a "spiritual" relationship with God. The liturgy of the future will have to remain aware of this basically human character of the liturgy. Insofar as God is at the origin of every human step toward God, the liturgy is inspired by God; but its exercise concerns the rhythm of life in the present, the rhythm of the human, in its bodiliness and its signifying activity of giving meaning. This is what led people to ask the Curé of Ars on his deathbed if he had any regrets before he died. His answer was, "I am sorry that in heaven we cannot 'communicate' [receive the eucharist]." Speaking of the "heavenly liturgy" is a type of anthropomorphism that tends to humanize what is beyond, as when we speak of God as "father" or "mother."

What we have heard, what we have seen with our eyes, what we have looked at and touched with our hands, concerning the word of life . . . we declare to you what we have seen and heard (1 Jn 1:1, 3).

The liturgy is the favored place where the community of believers gives this witness and makes this announcement with its sight, its taste, and its touching. The liturgy is a place where the senses of sight, hearing, touch, smell, and taste determine the objects, arrange the space, organize the relationship and the contact among persons. If someone puts water on our head for baptism, it is because we have a body that, being covered with soot, gets dirty and needs to be washed. If we eat and drink at the eucharist, it is because our survival depends on the meal. The liturgy involves seeing, hearing, and tasting because it concerns people.

To shed some light on the human dimension in Christian liturgy, I will begin by deriving a certain explanation of the human from the cultures of Black Africa that exalt humanity as the very place of the presence or activity of the sacred. Then I will analyze the marks of the human on the Christian liturgy, such as the visibility of the forms, the link to space and time as well as to the cultures of humanity, the bond to the community, and the symbolic aspects. These implications derive from the human imprint on liturgy and explain why rites have changed and are changing in Africa today, when the African human being is taken into account.

THE HUMAN IN THE SACRED,
OR VINDICATION OF THE HUMAN

"In spite of faith in the incarnation of God himself in Jesus, Christianity has never truly freed itself, it seems, from that suspicion about the body and about what can be sensed."[1] This suspicion goes back a long way, probably even to the roots of Western thought with Plato and Aristotle, for whom the best form of life is that "where there is no place either for joy or for pain, but only for thought at the highest possible degree of purity."[2]

No doubt linguistic philosophy, existentialism, and the deeper understanding of the laws of anthropology and of their involvement in all human actions convinced the West that it was necessary to abandon the classic dualism between body and spirit, and increasingly to affirm the indissoluble character of body and spirit, while at the same time distinguishing one from the other. A good example of this may be seen in the attempts of F. Marty to define a human being as a "signifying body,"[3] or again in theology, the consideration given to sensibility and, more widely, to bodiliness.[4] Paul De Clerck is right when he writes humorously: "The Christian liturgy is not Cartesian."[5] But this must still be brought together in practice.

Black Africa, in its view of the world and of life, and notably in its animism, has always denied a dichotomy within human nature and even within the universe, considering a human being as a microcosm, a universe in miniature, the bearer of the present and the future, of the here below and the beyond, of the visible and the invisible. In a human being—a veritable summary of the universe—we find earth and water, air and fire, perfume and stench, immanence and transcendence. The trance of the rites of healing or divination can be explained only by the fact that—in the human person—"natural" and "supernatural" touch. The human person already forms part of the "sacred"; he or she is even the figure of the divine.

Contempt for the body has not tainted African traditions. For them, to save an individual is to save body and spirit together. A human being is entirely in a fingernail, a hair, a flake of skin. We Africans do not look for the sacred farther away than in human beings. The veneration of a dead father, for instance, is not so much in the care given to his tomb, but above all in the elders who remain as living signs of his presence. The sacred reveals itself in procreation, especially in the mystery of woman as the being who communes more deeply with nature in the creation of life, in the dance that imitates and reproduces the rhythm of the universe. Anywhere there is a "rupture" of established patterns—where what appears suggests and sends us back to what does not appear—there we find the sacred.

Indeed, the sacred presents itself exactly as a break from what is ordinary, both in space and in time. This rupture is made concrete by a cessation of ordinary activities, a change of place or language or clothing. The sacred allows transcendence, the supernatural, the timeless to break into the tangible present.

In Christianity, revelation improves upon this in a striking way by informing us that humanity is created "in the image of God" (Gn 1:27). Christ is the Word who was made flesh (Jn 1:14), God become man. The man Jesus is the "image of the invisible God" (Col 1:15). By his death and resurrection he makes us sharers in the nature of God (2 Pt 1:4); we are a letter "written not with ink but with the Spirit . . . on tablets of human hearts (2 Cor 3:3).

Thus the human is in the sacred and the sacred in the human. All that is human can become a reason for praise and a place of epiphany and of glorifying God. The opposition between the human and the divine, between the sacred and the profane, between the natural and the supernatural, ultimately has its origin in paganism. Christian revelation has always held the two united, even while it distinguishes them in order to understand them better.

When we say "we're only human," we usually mean that we are weak and that forgiveness is needed for our sins. Nevertheless, the human has a right to hold its head high, for it is in the human that the divine is revealed, just as in the body our spirit is revealed.

Humanity is the road of God and of the church. Humankind "is the primary route that the Church must travel in fulfilling her mission . . . *the primary and fundamental way for the Church,* the way traced out by Christ Himself, the way that leads invariably through the mystery of the Incarnation and the Redemption."[6] Humanity is therefore sacred by virtue of being the *locus* for God's self-revelation. Are human beings not God's image and likeness? Again, has not Jesus given even his life for humankind (Jn 10:15)? Is there greater love than giving our life for those we love (Jn 15:13)? Humanity is the sacred par excellence because God's Son, Jesus, has given his life for the sake of humankind.

RITE AND HUMANITY

In the somewhat elaborate language of scholarship, a *rite* is a symbolic act attached to common or specific social processes, in a given time and space, to attain a result that transcends the totality of the elements set in motion, and which, beyond any specific benefit, embraces the mystery of human existence, which moves to its fulfillment in communion with the cosmos or with Being, with the divinity or the Transcendent.[7]

Is not a person body and spirit, a natural and supernatural being who is continually drawn toward the fullness of life? Accordingly, religious ritual moves toward saving life by means of continued and repeated acts. It picks up the codes of a species and a society while adapting to each new milieu of that species. Ritual reflects a totality of life that becomes familiar and disappears, and is simultaneously visible and invisible. Ritual is replete with symbols that simultaneously veil and unveil a deeper dimension and can move us to search further, to go beyond all our empirical discoveries. "Ritual starts procedures in order to climb a mountain from which we can see the heights, though we never put our physical foot on the mountain peak. Like Moses, ritual leads the people toward the Promised Land, but doesn't enter that place itself."[8] Humans are made in this way, always searching beyond themselves.

Still the question arises: Does ritual reflect reality or a mirage? For the one with eyes to see and ears to hear, the question seems strange, for what ritual makes present helps express the start of the process of "going beyond" appearances. And experience will never lose its value, because it serves as an indispensable reference point in ongoing stages of the path toward the infinite.

The person who celebrates is involved in an action that transcends the empirical person, because this subject is in relationship with the Transcendent. The question in play is one of *salvation*, that is, a search for the fulfillment and the fullness of life. The rite thus appears as a vehicle containing human life in its completeness and at the same time enables individual human beings to "accomplish" transcendence. For this reason the rite reflects human life and is deeply marked by it. The first mark left by a human being on the rite is his or her actions—to come together in a group, to move, to raise hands, to crouch, to prostrate oneself, to call on God, to speak, to offer, to sacrifice, to eat and drink. All such actions connote particular meanings within a given society. To be efficacious, ritual actions are worn like clothing and dwelt in by the person who performs them.

BODY AND COMMUNITY

The fact that it is a *human* being who celebrates imposes on liturgy the need to be embodied in visible, sensible forms. A human being is a "signifying body" situated in time and space. It is necessary that humans see forms and colors, and that they contemplate the glory of God in art, for God has torn the veil that covered all the peoples (Is 25:7). It is necessary for us to hear sounds and words, for the Son of God himself has become Word and has lived in our words, in order to speak to us. It is necessary for us to taste the flavor of God in God's gifts, appetizers for the feast that God prepares for all the peoples on the holy mountain, a feast of rich meats and fine wines (Is 25:6). It is necessary for us to savor sweet odors in order to be able to guess at the delights of the presence of God; we touch the holiness of God by embracing God's altars and the icons of God's glory in the saints and by taking off our shoes in the places where God is revealed (Ex 3:5).

In our age, though, we are in an odd position in relation to ritual. We have shortened (perhaps even suppressed) processions because we "don't have the time" or to avoid the "triumphalism of the Middle Ages." Have we lost something in the process, something that only a day of processional ritual can mediate? By limiting the liturgy of the word to reading and commenting discursively on scripture passages, do we exploit fully the riches of language? Does its power not go far beyond written texts and discursive commentaries?

Oral cultures present rich ways in which to proclaim a message: the short story, the narrative, mime, and drama. Eating and drinking are so minimalized in our celebrations that we desiccate their power in flat liturgy.

The fact that it is a *human* being that celebrates, furthermore, imposes on liturgy the need for inculturation. There is no such thing as a universal person. The universal is a conceptual notion required for abstracting and reasoning. But if we forget that the universal has no existence outside concrete subjects and individuals, the movement of the Spirit ends by losing its goal, which is to reach individuals in their particular circumstances. Each human being and culture has something unique, something that cannot be passed on to anyone else, even if they are similar to others.

Biologically, each of us is unique, despite the quantity of hereditary material we carry with us, despite the conditioning of the milieux where we evolve. God become human had to be born in space and time, in a specific people and race. This does not make of *those* conditions obligatory paradigms or paths for all other spaces and times but simply reflects a basic fact of human life.

The tendency toward uniformity and centralization, from Charlemagne to the Council of Trent, has never served well the cause of Christian liturgy, especially when this tendency came from an external power and from a culture foreign to the groups upon whom foreign forms of celebration were imposed. Instead, *diversification* of liturgical expression is the normal path taken as liturgies grow and spread, if external forms are not imposed.

The only truly Christian path to the God is by way of the dangerous encounter with the faces of all humankind, both a trial and a grace for a race of pilgrims that finds at every turn of the road new faces and new cultures in which the Christian message can deepen and develop along new lines.[9]

The search to impose uniformity reveals a temptation to pride, which makes a group in power pretend to possess God fully and to be able to impose limits on how God is revealed in "other" cultures. The diversities of liturgies can save us and make us touch the ineffable character of God and the divine mystery and to respect it in every people. When the Catholic church in Rome changes the title of the *Zairian Rite of Mass* into *The Roman Missal for Dioceses in Zaire*, it says that the church accepts Zairians in Catholicity only as Romans of Zaire.

Because of the human person who celebrates and that person's profoundly social nature, liturgy takes on a communal character, because persons function as human beings only through and in a community. The communal character of Christian liturgy comes from the fact that it is a "public service," "the Church's worship," "the Church's divine service."[10] But the communal character of liturgy also comes from the fact that this worship is offered by human beings. In reality, when humans carry out an important activity, they are involved in a set of circumstances that gives numerous options. This open-endedness assures a great number of opportunities, and is the community that creates human beings. An individual becomes human only in relationship to others. "The individual is a signifying body only by being at once a member of a social body."[11]

In Black African cultures, a person is nothing without the community. An individual becomes a person only by discovering herself or himself to be the child, husband or wife, father or mother of someone else. A single life is a bundle of relationships, a chain of alliances. One lives as a vessel linked to other vessels, which communicate among themselves. All that concerns life and its growth calls for harmonization, communion, and gathering of the life force of many individuals. A worship service, where the forces of transcendence and immanence interact, demands the presence of community—a community made up not only of those living on earth but equally of those living beyond the visible dimension of ordinary life.

Having recognized the communal character of humanity, we must also recognize that the periods in history when individualism has triumphed correspond to those when the liturgy dwindled. Josef Jungmann observes: "We have just completed several centuries famous for individualism; it would have been quite astonishing if the liturgy had flourished during that period."[12] On the other hand, we see that where the sense of community is liveliest, for instance, in the societies of Black Africa, liturgy flourishes and its power to attract continues to grow.

SIGNS AND SYMBOLS

Another dimension of the human in the liturgy derives from its symbolic character; a human being is an arch-symbol, a signifying body, a being who is visible and invisible at the same time. We have shown the human being in its link with the rite. What does the symbolic character mean? Liturgy will be the favored place for signs and symbols, a place suggesting the holy and not making it simply transparent, a place where nothing occurs without reason and always to signify the glory of God and the salvation of humanity. Since the human who celebrates is the image of God, liturgy is the antechamber of Mystery.

Let us not hurry to eliminate symbols under the pretext of simplifying liturgies. Without doubt, certain symbols no longer speak in a given age or cultural space. But we should not suppress these symbols without replacing them with others that speak more clearly. If a better symbol is not available, it is important not to leave a vacuum. The absence of symbol ruins the flow of liturgy. A symbol does not satisfy the worshiper, but provides a place where hunger grows, where thirst is aroused, and where the desire to go deeper grows.

Finally, liturgy must do justice to humanity: to the individual body, to the social body, and to the cosmic body of humanity. To do justice to the "body" in liturgy means to act so that the story of the human being who celebrates and the cosmic web that enfolds the person may become the *locus* of "spiritual" relationship and communion between humanity and God.

The movement of the incarnation—a unique fact in the history of religions—is sufficient to make us understand how vital is humanity's stake in its relationship with God. Our entire range of emotion and feeling is included in this relationship and contributes to the contact with God in liturgy and to the cohesion of each member of the assembly in the social body. The fact that the cultures of Black Africa take the body into account has helped me to understand more fully the anthropological axis of the rites and better to bring into relief the imprint of the human on the liturgy.

Liturgy is ideally at one moment the mirror of God and of humanity. But a certain kind of yesterday's liturgy too often emphasized the dimension of the divine to the extent of obscuring the human. The rediscovery of the complexity of human experience permits us to understand that bodiliness requires theological consideration, minimally because our embodied persons are where the Spirit is active. Christ says: "The hour is coming when you will worship the Father neither on this mountain nor in Jerusalem. . . . The true worshipers will worship the Father in spirit and truth" (Jn 4:21, 23). "Spirit and truth" should not be understood in the sense of the classic dualism of "matter-spirit," but rather in the perspective of a life devoted to doing the will of God, a life of a human being, in all its dimensions.

2

Baptism and Confirmation

In approaching experiences of sacramental inculturation, two questions arise. What is the unity among the sacraments? And, how many sacraments are there? The sacraments depend on one another as the expression of the gift of the life of Christ for the salvation of humanity. The paschal mystery is both the origin and the end of the sacraments. The water and the blood that ran from Christ's side on the cross gave birth to the sacraments. Both acts have the same purpose—to nourish human life. This unity is such that if one sacrament limps all limp. So too inculturation occurs throughout the *whole* sacramental system, and if it is reined in prematurely or takes place badly, the whole of Christian life limps.

The notion of a sign or a symbol has aided our generation to better understand that a sacrament is a "symbolic act,"[1] an act using the symbolic language of the church and immersed in the salvation brought by Christ. Sacraments are effective in the way that symbols contain in themselves their objects. As "memorial" of the action of Christ and of the whole of Christ's life as Word of life, gift of self, and praise of the Father, what is important is that they signify salvation in Christ. Whether there are seven or more is less important than that they signify this salvation in Christ. The physical "water and blood" that flowed at Calvary (Jn 19:34)—tiny stream that they were—become a cosmic torrent of new life (Ez 47). Christians who come to drink discover new harmony and quench their thirst. For the Jews, the number seven was a symbol of totality, not a mere numerical limit. In the conversation that this book initiates, I ask the reader to consider whether it is possible for new significant realities to appear in the life of one Christian community or another, such as the religious consecration in Africa, which would appear as sacrament signifying the radicality of the gospel; such as the celebration of mourning in Africa, as sacrament signifying the compassion of God for those who have lost somebody among their family.

THE HISTORICAL SEPARATION OF BAPTISM,
CONFIRMATION, AND EUCHARIST

From the beginning of the third century baptism and confirmation were usually conferred at the same ceremony during the Easter Vigil. They found their crowning moment in the eucharist. These rites together were called *mysteries,* following the example of the pagan rites in which initiates were drawn into communion with the gods by participating in their divine life. Thus, for example, there were "mysteries of Eleusis" and "mysteries of Isis and Osiris." During these rites there was talk about "illumination," "new understanding," and "rebirth." In time, these terms were used by Christians.

Using the terminology of "initiation," Christians will understand the transformation to be a change of being, as the pagan becomes a Christian, a child of God. This will occur instantly, the night of Easter. The Christians will also use this term to mark the unity of the three rites: immersion, anointing with "chrism," and communion at the table of the Lord. Christ is termed the foundation and crown of the new life. While pagan rites produced divine life according to human will, Christians understood themselves as receiving such effects only through the one who calls them and gives them life.

In the West, the unity of the three sacraments in one rite did not last. Confirmation was eventually reserved to the bishop and came to take place much later in the life of the Christian. Its character was altered because the bishop was often separated from many Christian communities and could come only occasionally. The East resolved the problem by authorizing each priest to confer confirmation, stipulating however that he use oil that had been consecrated by the bishop. Many historians think that the necessity of further catechesis of the young in the West led to the delay in the reception of the sacrament of confirmation and eucharist until the age of reason.

During the first centuries the most frequent form of baptism was of adults. It had three stages: a long preparation, an intermediate preparation, and the paschal vigil. The preparation involved an examination of candidates and their sponsors, including discussing whether their chosen line of work was compatible with the Christian life. There followed instruction in the scriptures, on Christian morality, and on the history of salvation. After these instructions, there was the laying on of hands on the catechumens.

Intermediate preparation coincided with Lent. In this way the entire church accompanied the catechumens in their journey of faith. This stage began with the inscription of names in the book of the church, multiple exorcisms, the imposition of hands, calling upon the Holy Spirit, tasting salt, and signing and anointing the senses. There were also instructions on the Creed and on the prayers, in particular the Our Father and Psalm 23. Finally, there was a rite of the renunciation of Satan accompanied by a statement of faith in Christ by the recitation of the Creed.

On the night of initiation catechumens were first brought into the baptistry, where they disposed of their clothes. Their bodies were anointed with oil. They were plunged into a font filled with water, and as they left the bath they were dressed in white robes. They were brought before the bishop, who anointed them with a fragrant oil and imposed hands on them as he asked that they receive the gift of the Holy Spirit. Finally, they sang Psalm 23 and were brought to the eucharistic table to share in the Lord's supper.

The significance of the actions is emphasized. The exorcisms make it known that God alone saves. It is God who delivers us from slavery. Human effort is only secondary. The oil used prior to the bath prepares the neophyte for battle, for the neophyte will now slip through the hands of the enemy. Water symbolizes purification and life. The pits of water and the act of plunging signify death and the tomb. The exit from the water symbolizes the resurrection, while the perfumed oil and the imposition of hands are signs of the commitment to the mission of the church.

While there were many elements of the baptismal rite that were practiced uniformly, in particular those described above, there were also differences. In Antioch, Jerusalem, and Milan, differences existed in relation to the practice of the imposition of hands and the unctions. The number of unctions varied from church to church. Some evidence suggests that the imposition of hands was performed after the rite of water, while others indicate that it was before the rite of water during the rites of exorcism.

The rite of baptism of infants grew more frequent after the sixth century in the West. Adult baptism was virtually eliminated, as most were baptized as infants. There was also a shift away from the death-to-life symbolism of total immersion. The separate stages disappeared and a multitude of secondary rites developed primarily because of the West's celebration of confirmation. Vatican II restored the rite of baptism for adults to a place of prominence and instituted the programs that eventually became the Rite of Christian Initiation for Adults. The teaching of Vatican II also emphasized the unity of the three sacraments and recommended that they be administered together for adults. This reinforced the relationship of baptism to Easter, and established Easter, in particular, and Sunday, secondarily, as the proper day for baptism. The teachings of Vatican II also emphasized the importance of baptism as a rite that occurs within the community, while the community is at prayer.

After Vatican II, article 65 of the *Constitution on the Sacred Liturgy* permitted the introduction of other elements of initiation into baptism, as long as they are native to a people and are not allowed to dominate the celebration of the Christian mystery. This has allowed pastors to retrieve ancient rites of initiation and make them "sacramentals" of the rite of confirmation. In this restored unity of initiation rites, confirmation takes place following the Roman ritual, but after the celebration certain ancestral rites may be added. Such rites are to be constructed to conform to the dictates of the *Constitution on the Sacred Liturgy* so that no element incorporated undermines the strength and centrality of the Christian meaning.[2] Despite this opening the Christian rite and ritual additions, such as those common in Africa, take place on parallel tracks rather than as parts of a unified whole.

THE RANZINNI-OUEDRAOGO SYNTHESIS

A tentative synthesis—developed in Mossi around the year 1971 by Camille Ranzinni and Robert Ouedraogo, who inaugurated it—followed a model similar to the way a family welcomes guests. This was combined with traditional elements of initiation. Two months before Easter the five stages of baptism began.

1. Initiation

A delegation accompanies the candidates to the door of the church. I give below a portion of their welcoming address:

> These individuals from the outside say that they have come so that we may ask that the head of the family present their request to enter here.
>
> And they also told us, "When someone wants to work, they begin by asking what their profit will be." They have asked us and we have answered them, "Those who come here receive the good news of Christ who is proclaimed. The good news enters the ears, then travels to the heart and fills it and all of their interior, and one is thus filled. When the interior is full, hunger ceases."
>
> And we have told them that when they have this happiness it is still not the real happiness. Christ will prepare for them a place in his native country. That is why the heart is no longer troubled, for there is nothing left to fear.
>
> And we have asked them, "You who see the effort that must be made, will you follow the path that they have taken? You have said that you will. But have you no concern that you will fall back and live as you did before?" They have said no, they will not return to their old ways.
>
> And this is why we have taken this upon ourselves. Our heart is firm, because when someone counts on you, you must do everything in your power not to let them down. That is what has brought us here today, and that is why we ask permission of the head of

the family. If you agree, then it is you who are the master of your work.[3]

After a brief exchange, the head of the family (in this case the priest) responds, pointing out to the sponsors their responsibilities. An exorcism accompanied by a sign of the cross takes place. The godparent, called "the father of baptism," gives the new name chosen from among African or Christian names. Finally, the community is questioned as to whether it gives its approval to welcome these invited guests into the family. The community says yes, and the catechumens are accompanied across the threshold of the church. They advance singing Psalm 23. The celebration continues with the liturgy of the word and the offerings.

2. Learning the Customs of Christians

The catechumens sing to express their desire to be initiated into the ways of the Christians: "Show me, because I am a stranger . . . a stranger does not know the way through the bog . . . show me." They kneel, elbows on the ground; godparents impose hands, after which follows an exorcism by the priest. The next part of the ritual is the gift of the bible. Those being initiated advance in procession to touch the bible with both hands and then receive the gift of the Creed and Our Father.

3. Gestures

The third stage, which takes place on Holy Thursday, is punctuated with three gestures: (1) the *epheta* ("be opened"), which is performed by the godparent on the godchild; the surrender of the old ways and the name; and the recitation of the Creed and the Our Father. (2) The catechumens come forward carrying small pieces of paper bearing their names; these they throw into a pit, cut in the shape of a Mossi tomb, between the catechumens and the ministers. (3) Finally, the catechumens turn eastward.

4. Mourning

Mourning also takes place on Holy Thursday. First, there is a Mossi funeral procession in which the cross is carried, balanced as if it were a body; this is accompanied with weeping and wailing. Second, the catechumens straddle the cross in a traditional expression of fidelity (where the oldest son straddles the body of his dead father to symbolize his faithfulness to the family). In traditional African culture this a moment of solemn commitment; the rite of baptism is portrayed as a similar solemn commitment for life.

5. Bathing and Anointing

The last stage of initiating begins at the Easter Vigil. It is inaugurated when the new fire is lighted in a circular hole dug on Good Friday. With the community gathered around the fire, the enthronement of Christ is proclaimed and three healing names attributed to Christ are called out, first in a whisper, and then louder and louder, until they are sung in full voice with the sound of instruments and gunfire in the background. Jars of water placed around the hole are then blessed. The invocation of Christian ancestors or saints follows. Finally, the heads of the catechumens are bathed in water and anointed with holy oils.

THE SANON SYNTHESIS

Monsignor A. T. Sanon's experimental rite approaches a synthesis in four stages: (1) each catechumen speaks about what he or she formerly believed; (2) an exorcism is performed; (3) a new mask is given; and (4) wearing this mask, each catechumen chooses the sign of a new secret.

On the same day stories are told of the foreshadowing of Jesus and his saving passion and death in the Old Testament. The Christian saints are recognized as new ancestors (i.e., of the African people), and the revelation and inscription of a new name in the community records takes place. The Our Father and the Creed are said; baptism and confirmation follow, ending with the celebration of the eucharist. Later, doctrinal formation will take place in several stages.[4]

One sees in these examples that in fact the content of the traditional African rites of initiation has been removed and replaced with the faith of the community in Christ. "To be initiated is to join in his initiation by taking part in the trials [of Jesus Christ]. The principal element of initiation involves giving oneself up, giving one's life in loving service. This shows us the way of initiation, which one can follow to the end just as he [Jesus Christ] did."[5]

THE DIOCESE OF DIEBOUGOU

The same perspective can be found in the stages of baptism in the diocese of Diebougou.[6] The stages contain traditional initiation elements, such as the announcement of initiation, reciting the history of the family, and a dance by the initiates to end each stage of the process. Again we see that the rituals have been emptied of traditional meaning. They have become a backdrop for the enactment of a new play. Implied in this is the judgment that Africans had to reject the content of traditional initiation as if it were in contradiction to the Christian message. Rather, one must discover the way in which the traditional meaning of initiation reveals at its heart the evangelical message. Then the Christian rite can bless those values through the grace of the salvation in Jesus Christ.

THE TSHIKAPA-KELE EXPERIENCE

One attempt moving in this direction can be found in Tshikapa-Kele, led by Abbot Ntumba-Mweza-Mwanza. The catechumens retire with the initiators into the forest for a week. There the traditional rite of initiation takes place. It includes tests; teaching of Bantu traditions and religious values; instruction in the Christian faith and traditional rites; all culminating in baptism, confirmation, and eucharist in the parish church.

CIJIBA

In Cijiba a fairly unified ritual has begun that is rooted in the gathering of communities. It is first of all for adults and is based in the new Roman rite's permission for the conferral of baptism, confirmation, and eucharist in one ceremony in the initiation of adults. The ceremony is on Holy Saturday during the Easter Vigil because that moment affords the best occasion to absorb the meaning of the paschal mystery. Because the rite is for adults, the traditional rite of initiation has already begun and it continues. In effect, the harmonization of the life by rites, determined by the way in which an infant is brought into the world, continues to mark the life of the individual. For instance, it is significant whether the head or arm comes first from the womb; whether the umbilical cord is wrapped around the waist; whether a boy is born after three, five, or seven girls (or the opposite); whether twins are born; or whether the child was conceived before the mother's menstrual cycles returned after a previous childbirth. Rites relative to the entry into a profession or into marriage also continue. African Christians are allowed to continue such traditions as long as they eliminate what is contrary to love of God and love of neighbor.

Baptism is a threshold to a new potentiality of being because it solemnizes and marks the encounter of the catechumen with Jesus Christ. This requires a characteristic *Christian* rite of passage linked with traditional community rites of initiation. The drama of life of Africans is therefore integrated into Christian baptism according to the following, four-element schema:

1. Seclusion

For the last two weeks of Lent, catechumens retire from ordinary life. They come and stay at the church, men on one side and women on the other. They follow a program of intensive prayer based on the liturgy of the hours—matins, lauds with meditation, office of readings at the beginning of the afternoon, the eucharist celebrated just before sunset, and, before going to bed, compline. These offices have been translated into the native language.

2. Asceticism

The catechumens give themselves to hard work under the direction of different parish committees. The committee on development and health trains them in areas such as the cultivation of common fields and the maintenance of public places such as the maternity ward and the dispensary. They are educated in new skills, including the culinary arts and the way to purify water.

3. Religious Instruction

Those present, of course, have already received religious instructions in their communities from elders and catechists. During this time of seclusion, afternoons are devoted to deepening that faith. The parish committees on inculturating the gospel and on catechesis and liturgy take charge. The first committee begins with the history of the peoples; it explains the mores and customs of the ancestors related to the human life cycle from birth to death. These customs are discussed in relation to the Christian way of life and faith. The committee on catechesis follows with the history of salvation and the mysteries of faith (the Creed). The instruction is linked with that of the commission on liturgy and its efforts to initiate the catechumens into the cultic life of Christians. Each day they participate in the eucharist.

4. Celebrating the Rites of Initiation

During the night of Holy Saturday—after the liturgy of light, the readings, the homily, the proclamation of faith and the renunciation of Satan—there follows the reenactment of the death and resurrection of Christ. The candidates are made to crouch on the floor and are covered with banana leaves, as if they were dead. A chant of mourning is intoned, including this traditional refrain:

> Here is Muswamba, child of Kalunda,
> she was dead, and yet she seems to sleep.

Or there is simply a moment of silence, following which the priest takes the right arm of the candidate and lifts her or him up saying in a loud voice:

> Christ has left the tomb, and lives forever;
> You too, live with him. Stand up.

Verses 15, 16, and 17 of Psalm 118 are then sung:

The right hand of the LORD does valiantly,
the right hand of the LORD is exalted,
the right hand of the LORD does valiantly,
I shall not die, but I shall live,
and recount the deeds of the LORD.

After this comes the bathing of the head with water and the invocation of the Trinity. The priest incenses the candidates and calls the baptized by their new names. Names are chosen to recall or express devotion to a Christian saint or a mystery of salvation in Christ or sometimes even the name of one of the traditional ancestors—under the condition that this name is joined in relationship with God. (If the reader recalls the quarrel between the Zairian bishops and the Mobutu regime in 1972, it was over the issue of first names. The new government had removed foreign names from all identity cards as part of the regime's effort to return to "authentic" African culture. That same year, while affirming the right of Christians to adopt a name that recalled a Christian saint, the church permitted ancestral names to be used as baptismal names, as long as they were held to be in relation to the gift of God.[7])

In the early church Christians did not change their names at baptism. Rather, it was a practice in the synagogues that the proselytes would take a Jewish name in identification with the community that had welcomed them. As pagans were baptized, certain Jewish-Christians began having these initiates change their names to share in the spirit of different Christians, alive or dead. In this way, for example, Cyprian took the name Cecilius because he had accompanied him on his journey toward conversion. Eusebius the historian added Pamphilos to his name in recognition of this martyr. St. Ignatius of Antioch at his baptism took the name of Theophoros. This practice of taking the names of apostles or martyrs dates to the third century and was used for individuals or assigned at the baptism of an infant. The bishops of Congo (Zaire), it should be observed, did not begin this practice. The political intervention of the government had been in fact beneficial for the conclusion of the question of names for baptism.

The rite of naming takes place by the priest asking the godparent for the godchild's name. The godparent responds with a recitation of the godchild's genealogies, after which the chosen name is given as the crowning of the catechumen's identity. When he finishes, the priest offers a special greeting to the baptized by solemnly pronouncing the new name and shaking the newly baptized person's hand.

Then comes the anointing of confirmation. Before proceeding, the priest invites the godparent to accompany the godchild on the spiritual journey. The godparent carries the articles necessary for the godchild's profession and his or her own, and he or she dances with these articles.

They are presented to the priest, who blesses them, after which the priest anoints the newly baptized and lays hands on him or her.

Finally, the celebrant puts a bit of white kaolin (chalk) on the arms, cheeks, and feet of the initiate, saying that he or she is a new being and that he or she has achieved a new stature in the church. The celebrant shakes the new members' hands and presents each one to the assembly saying:

> Just as Christ passed from this world to the Father, so N. has moved from slavery of sin to liberation, from death to life. What has been accomplished for him (her) is what we must live, for we have been baptized, too. For having been victorious with Christ, let us applaud N. with great jubilation.

The congregation sings a joyful song and an Alleluia. Offerings are made and the eucharist follows, during which the newly baptized come to the Lord's eucharistic table.

3

The Eucharist

The central themes of this chapter circle around the need to link sacramental re-presentation of the paschal mystery of Christ with the rhythms of African life and culture. Accordingly, celebrating the eucharist in Black Africa is above all to proclaim and make present salvation for black Africans through the death and resurrection of Jesus Christ by having them hear the word and receive the body and blood of Jesus in the way that Jesus has instructed us to do. But the words and deeds of Jesus are not fixed like stones. They are alive. The dynamic reality of a God who has become human joins black Africans in the immediate present of their situation, to enliven the interior and let it shine forth, so that they can glorify God in the depths of their souls. Their oral genius, spiritual vitality, dance, signs, and symbols must proclaim that Jesus Christ is Savior.

Black Africans consider themselves as "oaks grown from ancient stumps"; they are like grafted branches that continue to be nourished by the roots of an ancient tree. If Jesus brings them back to life, his action will also touch the ancestors, who are the channels by which the movement of life continues its course, moving from its source toward its destiny. That is why at the Christian eucharist of Black Africa the ancestors are integrated in the invocations and symbolic libations.

The orders of worship in these rituals are complex because they attempt to combine harmoniously the Christian rubrics of the celebration, the structure of an assembly around the chief (is not the eucharist the place where we are called by God and assembled around the Lord Jesus?), on the one hand. And on the other hand, they do not hesitate to incorporate the initiation rites of passage and the communal meals around the tree of the ancestors.

Finally, celebrating the eucharist in Black Africa with the local food and drink in a land that has neither wheat nor vineyards is to make this local nourishment and drink a place of the epiphany of the Lord's own meal and the proclamation of his death and resurrection. On the table of

the disciples at Emmaus Jesus did not take out his own sandwich or pic-
nic lunch. He took what the disciples had with them. He ate it in a new
way that proclaimed his death and resurrection.

EUCHARIST WITHIN THE CHRISTIAN TRADITION

We find in the New Testament four versions relating to the first celebration of the eucharist. The similarities and differences within these
various texts reflect two traditions, first that of Mark and Matthew, second that of Luke and Paul. In Mark and Matthew these rites indicate
that the bread is broken and the cup is taken at the same time, during or
at the end of the meal. In Luke and Paul the breaking of the bread is done
before the meal, and the glass of wine is taken after the meal. The number of cups of wine is also not the same in the various traditions. Luke
records two cups, while the others only speak of one. Among the differences, it is also important to note that the command "do this in memory
of me" is only present in the last block (Paul and Luke). The following
are the key texts:

1. *Matthew 26:26-28*
    While they were eating, Jesus took a loaf of bread, and after
blessing it he broke it, gave it to his disciples and said, "Take, eat;
this is my body." Then he took a cup, and after giving thanks he
gave it to them, saying, "Drink from it, all of you; for this is my
blood of the covenant, which is poured out for many for the forgiveness of sins."

2. *Mark 14:22-24*
    While they were eating, he took a loaf of bread, and after bless-
ing it he broke it, gave it to them and said, "Take; this is my body."
Then he took a cup, and after giving thanks he gave it to them, and
all of them drank from it. He said to them, "This is my blood of the
covenant, which is poured out for many."

3. *Luke 22:14-20*
    When the hour came, he took his place at the table, and the
apostles with him. . . . Then he took a cup, and after giving thanks
he said, "Take this and divide it among yourselves; for I tell you
that from now on I will not drink of the fruit of the vine until the
kingdom of God comes. Then he took a loaf of bread, and when he
had given thanks, he broke it and gave it to them, saying, "This is
my body, which is given for you. Do this in remembrance of me."
And he did the same with the cup after supper, saying, "This cup
that is poured out for you is the new covenant in my blood."

4. 1 Corinthians 11:23-25

The Lord Jesus on the night when he was betrayed took a loaf of bread, and when he had given thanks, he broke it and said, "This is my body that is for you. Do this in remembrance of me." In the same way he took the cup also, after supper, saying, "This cup is the new covenant in my blood. Do this, as often as you drink it, in remembrance of me."

These verses reveal liturgical practices "performed well before being committed in writing and incorporated into the gospels."[1] They are among the first written biblical texts we have and are taken from the center of the Christ-kerygma, which interprets the paschal mystery as the death and resurrection of Jesus as the Christ.

Luke and Paul reflect the traditions of Greek communities or Christians living within a Hellenic milieu. Their vocabulary is typical of these environments. These communities maintained an ancient structure that was faithful to traditions of Jewish meal rituals. Here the blessing of bread comes before the meal and is followed by or interrupted with a blessing of wine. In Mark and Matthew, although an ancient vocabulary is used, it reflects a new structure. In it two rites are brought together and grouped at the end of the meal.

If we look at the background of the meal, it seems quite clear that the Jewish meal of Passover or other cultic feasts gave Jesus and later the first Christians a threefold model for interpreting and celebrating the achievement of salvation through his life and work.[2] What was this model?

First, there is an *entrance*. Participants wash their hands (rite of purification); they recline; a cup of wine is brought forward; the president or the head of the family receives it and pronounces the blessing: "Holy are you, our God, King of all ages, who has given us this fruit of the vine." He drinks the wine and the "hors d'oeuvres" are served.

Second, the meal is preceded by a *breaking of bread*. Before anyone eats, the presider or the head of the family takes the bread, pronounces the blessing, breaks it, and gives it to his guests. The blessing is stated in these terms: "Blessed are you, our God, King of all ages, you who have brought forth bread from the earth."

Third, there is a ritual revolving around the *cup of blessing*. The final courses are served, and before the end of the meal the cup is brought to the one presiding. That person takes the cup, elevates it slowly, and pronounces a triple blessing; the first resembles the preceding ones; the second begins with "We offer you praise . . . " and God is thanked for all of his wonders throughout salvation history; the third is a series of requests: "Have pity . . . feed your people . . . sustain your people . . . that your reign may be without end."

The Greek translation of "We offer you praise" in the second prayer is *eucharistoumen,* and the noun form of the word is *eucharistia,* the word that in time will come to serve to designate the whole rite. The Jewish Passover ritual, in other words, inspired Jesus, and the synoptic accounts of the Last Supper situate it in the midst of the Jewish Passover. The first Christians took the words and actions of Jesus and regarded them as the summit of the wonders of God, which are mentioned in the blessing. In the beginning it appears that they preserved the eucharist rites within the course of a meal; but even so, in certain communities, its separation was made necessary because of difficulties encountered and recorded in Paul's first letter to the Corinthians (11:17-34). Eventually the community meal took place before the rite.[3]

A study of the form of Jewish prayer on which Christian eucharistic practice rests indicates that the daily prayers of the synagogue were divided into three parts: (1) reading a passage from the Law; (2) reciting the *"shema* Israel" of Deuteronomy 6:4, "Hear, O Israel"; and (3) recounting the eighteen blessings (*Teffilah*). The reading of the Law was preceded by a recitation of psalms. The recitation of the *"shema* Israel" at morning prayer was preceded by a blessing concluded by the "Holy, Holy, Holy."[4]

> Blessed are you, Lord our God, King of the Universe, you who formed the light and created the darkness, who makes peace and created all things; who through your mercy give light to the earth, to all who inhabit it; in your goodness, renew creation every day and without cease. How numerous are your works, Lord. In your wisdom you made them all, the earth is full of your possessions; King who alone was exalted before time, praised, glorified, and exalted from the time immemorial. . . . The chiefs of the armies of God are saintly beings, they exalt the Almighty, without ceasing they declare the glory of God and his holiness. . . . And all of the spirits that serve him, are in the heavens of the universe, and with awe they proclaim in one, full voice the words of the living God, and of the eternal King. . . . In the peaceful joy of the spirit, in a pure language with a saintly melody, all respond in unison in awe and with reverence. . . . Holy, holy, holy, Lord God of hosts, the earth is filled with your glory.[5]

It is worthwhile to note common elements, for at the heart of the eucharistic rite of the first two centuries were (1) a rite centered on bread, (2) a rite centered on wine, (3) prayers of praise and thanksgiving centered on Jesus as the goal of the wonders of God, which are recalled in using Jewish blessings where the community praised God for who he has been and thanked God for what he has done on its behalf. This thanksgiving opens up into an eschatological supplication that remains the skeleton of our contemporary eucharistic prayer.

A broad overview of subsequent developments will establish the context for understanding African liturgy. In the second and third centuries one can distinguish the five following elements. First, *prayers of thanksgiving* are centered on Jesus as the ultimate wonder of God. Second, *words of institution* recall the death and resurrection of Jesus in the manner of a "memorial" (Dt 5:2-3) in the strong Hebrew sense of that word, that is to say the accomplishment or "real re-presentation" today of what occurred in the past. Third, an *eschatological supplication* wherein forgiveness of sins is requested, the dead are prayed for and God is asked to unite the entire community in the kingdom. Especially in the East, Christians developed this latter element around the role of the Spirit and saw the present as a time of pilgrimage on earth. Because of the Spirit's role in the eschatological dimension, this prayer was called the *epiclesis*. In the original form of certain Syrian documents it took the form of a request for the grace of God (or of the *Logos*) to gather the elect and make them a faithful people. To this a supplication for the acceptance of sacrifice was added, and this last element developed into a request for the consecration of gifts in combination with a request that the Holy Spirit make the gifts fruitful in the church for the praise of the Father.[6]

Fourth, there was the *offering*. By praying for grace, Christians offer to God the grace that they have received, that is to say the Christ, and themselves. It is at this level that the intercessions are introduced. Finally, the *doxologies*, which are found scattered throughout certain eucharistic prayers and are united in one place in others, celebrate God's glory. The doxologies reflect clearly the influence of Jewish blessings.

Those are the fundamental elements of the Christian eucharistic prayers. The order in which these elements occur may differ from church to church. Some eucharistic prayers may lack certain elements. After the year 350 C.E., four basic orientations are present: (1) the Western Syrian rite, developing around Antioch and Jerusalem, will give birth to the Byzantine rite in the Greek language; (2) the Eastern Syrian rite (the Chaldean rite) will crystallize around Edessa and in Mesopotamia in the Syriac language; (3) the Alexandrian rite will arise in Egypt and serve as a model for both Coptic and Ethiopian rites; (4) the Roman rite, beginning in Italy, will predominate in Gaul and Spain, where by the ninth century it will supplant the Gallican and the Mozarabic rites centered at Toledo and Braga.

Several factors influenced the development of these rites. First there were the natural geographic boundaries, the different Roman provinces that also marked the ecclesiastical provinces or patriarchies, each according to its culture. Three languages predominated: Syro-Aramaic (Jerusalem and Antioch), Greek (Alexandria), and Latin (Rome and the West). And christological disputes of the third century reinforced these divisions.

Development of liturgy, of course, did not stop in the sixth or seventh or eleventh or sixteenth century. The central point for this volume, however, is that the development of the Western, Latin, or Roman rite followed the pattern of earlier developments. That is to say, it occurred for complex historical, cultural, theological, and religious reasons, but its occurrence cannot be denied. We shall not go through all these developments but conclude this section with some reference to the development of the eucharistic liturgy in the reforms of Vatican II.

The Second Vatican Council accomplished major syntheses and retrieved important insights from other rites and other ages. For instance, it overcame the controversy between East and West by emphasizing the consecratory role of the words of institution more than the invocation of the Holy Spirit. But also, it developed new formulations of the *epiclesis*. It took into account the criticisms of Protestants by emphasizing in its prayers the unity of the sacramental with the one sacrifice of Jesus, showing that in the deepest sense of *memorial,* the unique sacrifice is re-presented. Also, without destroying the Roman rite, it revamped it so that its values (notions of offering and the divine presence) reemerged. It introduced a recollection of creation and the life communicated by the Spirit. It also composed new eucharistic prayers by drawing inspiration from other Christian traditions. Prayer II is very close to the Anaphora of Hippolytus, whereas III and IV follow the Syrian model. The developments of prayers of praise are situated in the terminology and the actual perspectives of the science of theology. In this way archaic forms are not simply reproduced; rather, new syntheses embrace the ancient traditions.

These changes did not solve the problem of liturgical reforms for places such as Africa, but the principle that change can and should occur to renew liturgical celebration was clearly laid down. Below we examine some of the results of that dynamic in Africa.

EUCHARIST FORMS FROM AFRICA

The first things that catch the eye are the forms, the vestments, the rhythm that animate eucharistic celebrations in Africa. Perhaps these are not the most important, but one must begin there, with the dance, the environment, a new language, and another way of ordering worship.

DANCE

In Black Africa, rhythm is supreme and is everywhere. The world moves in a rhythm. Seasons follow one another. Man and woman are born. They grow and die. They are carried by the rhythm. It is universal for humans to attempt to overcome anxiety by celebrating rites along stages in life's journey. In them we invoke the One who can master life in all its twists and turns.

Better still, we try to harmonize our lives with the rhythm of the universe. In Africa, in particular, it is characteristic to believe that the world is well-created and beats with a certain rhythm. Therefore, humans must synchronize themselves with this rhythm. This is the principal role of the dance. One dances in joy (*cyanga*) as certainly as one dances in pain; one dances love as certainly as one dances anger and hatred (*disempela,* as they call it in *Ciluba* language). One dances rest and work. All life's elements come from rhythm and harmony and are to be celebrated in dance. Accordingly, because one dances life, it is normal to dance the life in Jesus Christ, who is communicated to his followers in the liturgy. Prayer, being life, must be danced in Africa.[7]

In fact, ritual dance has always existed in human history, and not just in Africa. Oriental cults incorporated it. Judaism recognized it; many psalms encourage dancing: "Let us dance for our God, play for him tambourines and flutes, sound the horn." Did not King David dance before the ark of Yahweh while it was carried to Jerusalem (2 Sm 6:14)? The first Christians did not adopt dance as part of the liturgy. First of all, they sought to separate themselves from the Jews and, above all, did not want to resemble flamboyant pagan cults that often degenerated into drinking bouts and orgies and sometimes included trances under the effect of the music and the dance.[8]

By the Christian Middle Ages, moreover, a theology that held the body in contempt and that favored the spirit had triumphed. This theology was influenced by a dualistic conception of human personality as composed of a body and a soul, a conception that is not in fact biblically based. This theology inspired a piety that tended exclusively toward contemplation and toward a kind of prayer that ignored the body or sought liberation from it. Manuals of liturgical piety demanded that the faithful maintain a severe outward appearance.

In Black African civilization, on the other hand, the material universe is the place into which the divine irrupts. It is therefore the place of communion with the divine. The body necessarily forms part of the prayer. And since rhythm constitutes a fundamental reference to the intelligibility and experience of the universe, dance becomes a necessity for prayer. Above all, in the liturgy there exists a communion between forces of immanence and transcendence.

Although even in the West today the value of liturgical dance is being reevaluated, it is seen above all as movement that helps to express and communicate a message to spectators.[9] But even this is not widely accepted. In Africa, by contrast, one expresses oneself through dance, but above all, one seeks harmony between one's body and spirit in the liturgical action, harmony between the members and the community at prayer, harmony with the Spirit of God, which makes us pray. And thus one dances the eucharist.

NATURAL ENVIRONMENT AND LITURGY

In what follows we wish to discuss the fact that the natural environment is not a mere stage setting in liturgical celebration. In holistic liturgy symbols are not external and they are indispensable to underline different aspects of the central Christian message. We know that symbols are multivalent and complex and therefore always require explanation. This orientation toward meaning is essentially accomplished through the material environment of the symbol.

In a eucharistic celebration in Black Africa, the environment must symbolize what the eucharist represents—for instance, offering oneself to God, the praise of God, the passage from death to life, the victory of Christ over evil and death, the triumph of life over death. The eucharist is the place of communion between God and human beings, a place of communion among human beings, a place of intercession for the world. What symbols can portray this message best in Africa?

First of all, architecture must be endowed with African symbols. And for a church, the main entrance constructed in the shape of a mask would be quite suggestive; there are many masks of initiation that symbolize life, fertility, rebirth. The example of the facade of the church of Boni, the parish of Our Lady of Fatima in Burkina Faso, is one of the most successful. It represents a Bwa mask of initiation. As one enters the church, one senses being drawn into a place of fertility and rebirth.

A tree of life near the altar of eucharistic sacrifice, planted in a great earthen jar, reinforces the idea of the fruitfulness of the sacrifice and the idea that it procures life. The tree could be a banana tree, an "ancestral tree" (which is resistant to dryness), or even a tree with white bark, which symbolizes harmony, blessing.

In Tshikapa-Kele a hut dedicated to the ancestors is constructed at the foot of the altar. In front of this hut (which measures fifty centimeters in height and forty centimeters in width), a log burns throughout the celebration, and incense is thrown onto it from time to time. During the Malawian mass at Lilongwe, a similar fire is lighted next to the altar, and a person is charged with attending to it throughout the celebration. The altar is covered with a leopard skin, which is removed after the celebration.

Instead of a leopard skin, some churches place elephant tusks in front of the altar and the tabernacle. On the walls Bantu symbols of power and protection, such as triangles and spears, surround the tabernacle. On the liturgical vestments one finds designs marking fertility, as well as rings, spirals, pearls, and shells, signs of fertility and richness because worship is the place where life becomes fruitful and where we possess the veritable richness of our being.

The gourd on the table cover of the altar symbolizes mother-church. The miter of Cardinal Malula bore a knot, which indicated the dynamism of the Spirit that animated his ministry. As for colors, the trilogy of white-black-red mark the life. Ordinary worship of cult must bear all three colors. The white color used alone is always a sign of communion with the beyond, and it conforms perfectly with worship that is the place of contact with the supernatural. Among the Bantu white is also worn by those in mourning, not as a sign of sadness, but as a sign of the proximity of the beyond as a channel for approaching death, a death that is a door to the beyond. At Bantu Christian burials white is worn, inspired by the white band that is tied around the head of those who go to an interment. Sometimes one puts a black star on a white dawn to indicate the passage from death to life.

COMPLEX ORDERS OF WORSHIP

The African Independent Christian churches have preceded us in this research, but by and large they have developed mainly the liturgy of the word, inheritors as they were of the Protestant worship. For them, the Lord's supper is celebrated only three or four times a year, at major feasts or at special events in the life of the church. I give below a schema that corresponds in a general way to eucharists one can find in such churches as the Neo-apostolic, Twelve Apostles, Martyrs, Light, Pentecostal, Good News, and Church of the Good God. They entail:

Entrance and assembly hymns
Readings and announcements
Profession of faith
Purification rites (the majority of which are centered on sprinkling of holy water, the imposition of hands, and prayers of supplication)
Procession of gifts and offerings
Prayer of consecration over eucharist elements (which are different among the churches, some containing explicit references to the words of institution of the Lord's supper in the gospels)
Communion of the ministers and the faithful
Hymns and psalms of thanksgiving, and sometimes the Lord's Prayer
Blessing and dismissal

In Western Africa, in the worship of the church of the Lord Aladura, which takes its origins in Anglicanism, after the scriptural readings, preaching, and offerings, one moves on to the holy communion, which is comprised of a rubric mentioning who is worthy to participate in communion; the hymn "I am Hungry and Thirsty"; Psalm 51, which is followed by a prayer of absolution; the hymn "Here Is a Fountain Filled with Blood"; a sprinkling of holy water and formula for the absolution of sins; a prayer of consecration of the gifts of bread and wine; an account of the institution of the eucharist; the hymn "Come, the Feast is Ready"; distribution; a communion hymn; the prayer of conclusion and blessing.

Among the Kimbanguists—or the Church of Jesus Christ on Earth, founded by the prophet Simon Kimbangu—the worship of the Last Supper unfolds as follows: hymns; readings of the New and Old Testaments; prophecies; a prayer for the transformation of the elements; carrying the elements before the assembly; the pastor prays over those who will distribute the gifts; reading 1 Corinthians 11:13-29; two orations said by the pastor; the presider raises his hands and blesses the assembly; the people receive communion, and then those who distributed communion receive last; and finally a closing prayer is said by the presider.

This order was established in 1971, at the time of the consecration of the tomb of the prophet Simon Kimbangu at N'kamba, the place where his ministry had flourished in a special way.[10]

African Catholic Eucharists

Ndzon-Melen in Cameroon

In the Catholic church, the mass of Ndzon-Melen, a parish in a suburb of Yaoundé (Cameroon), first attracted attention in 1967. Because of this attention, this parish was invited to represent Africa at the Eucharistic Congress of Lourdes in 1982. The order of worship in this mass is divided into two principal parts: the acclamation of the book and readings, and the eucharistic meal. The structure has two basic elements, each of which is comprised of various rituals:

1. The Reading of the Word
   Hymns and dances
   Incensing the book of readings
   Procession with the book
   Enthronement of the book
   Solemn announcement of the theme of the gathering
   Readings from the Old and New Testament
   Homily
   Creed and collection
   Penitential rite and prayer of the faithful
2. The Meal
   Presentation of the offering within a dance
   Preface, *Sanctus*, first part of the Roman canon
   Gloria after the consecration of the gifts
   Remainder of canon, the Our Father, and Lamb of God
   Sign of peace and communion
   Songs and dances of thanksgiving
   Final prayer, blessing, and dismissal[11]

Zairian Rite

The experience of liturgical adaptation in Zaire began around the year 1969 under the direction of Laurent Mpongo of Zaire. Father Mpongo was well trained in liturgical studies, and he had come from the Liturgical Institute of Saint Anselm in Rome. He also filled the role of secretary of the Episcopal Commission on Evangelization for the Episcopal Conference of Zaire.

A first stage in the process of experimentation issued in a brochure "Towards an African Mass" in 1974. The second stage involved a series of meetings and negotiations between the episcopate of Zaire and Rome. These ended with an official promulgation on 30 April 1988 entitled "The Roman Missal for the Dioceses of Zaire." The structure of the liturgy follows this sequence:

Entrance procession
Veneration of the altar by the celebrant
Announcement of the theme of the celebration and greeting of the
    assembly by the celebrant
Invocation of the saints and ancestors
Song of praise danced around the altar
Opening prayer by the priest
Readings of the Old and New Testament
Procession with the gospel book
Proclamation of the gospel
Homily
Profession of Christian faith
Penitential rite, with or without sprinkling of holy water
Kiss of peace
Universal prayer
Collect and procession of gifts
Prayer over the offerings
Preface and canon (spoken in dialogue)
Our Father, Lamb of God, communion
Songs of thanksgiving
Prayer, blessing, dismissal

It is important to note that the role of the announcer is emphasized in the rite; he often intervenes to invite the people to worship, to explain what is happening in the liturgy, and so forth. This rite was conceived as a general framework, on the foundation of which regional and cultural differences will be added. Liturgical practices, the decoration of places, the dance steps that accompany different actions, gestures expressing worship, supplication, emotional movements toward God and other different possibilities offered through the languages of different regions give concreteness and particularity to different expressions of the same rite throughout the country.

As an example of this diversity, the invocation of the ancestors at Tshikapa-Kele, St. Joseph's "Bukidadidi" parish, is very different from the Kinshasa parishes. For Christians in Tshikapa, saying to the ancestors only "be with us" is not enough to invoke the ancestors at the beginning of the celebration. The weight and measure of their importance is far greater than that simple act. Instead, at Tshikapa, they choose extracts from the ancestors' words of wisdom, which shape the social fabric and orientation of our societies. These are taken as words preparing the encounter with God's word. Thus began the practice of offering a reading on the "wisdom of the ancestors" within the eucharistic liturgy. This practice brought about a restructuring of the lectionary and the liturgy of the word.[12]

At Cijiba, also in Kasayi, the official Zairian rite has inspired the following schema:

Entrance procession (song, dance, incensing of the altar)
Invocation of the ancestors of the region
Invocation of the ancestors of the country
Invocation of the ancestors of Africa
Invocation of saints
Song of praise to God (with incensing of the altar and dancing around it)
Prayer of the priest
Request and gift of white kaolin to the reader (gesture of blessing)
Readings
Procession of the gospel (displaying the book and dance, which accompany the Alleluia, incensing)
Gospel and homily
Christian profession of faith
Penitential rite with sprinkling of holy water
Gesture of peace (the community shakes hands)
Prayer of the faithful
Offerings and collect
Procession to the altar
Presentation
Hymn to Christ, *Sanctus*
Eucharistic prayer in dialogue
Breaking of the bread, *Agnus Dei*
Integration of the ancestors in the new communion: blessing of the "tree of the ancestors" with holy water, or placing the paten with the host under the tree of ancestors (the celebrant, who represents the new elder, will consume this host, after the communion of all the faithful)
Communion of the celebrant and the faithful
Moment of reflection in silence
Song of thanksgiving

Praise and Our Father
Blessing and dismissal

Malawian Mass

In Malawi the inculturation of Christian rites reaches a high level in the monastery of the Poor Clares of Lilongwe. Their way of life, their liturgical celebration of the hours, are, in my opinion, among the most successful attempts at inculturation of Christianity in Black Africa. Once or twice a year the Malawi Mass, which was born of their prayer and reflection through the rhythm of the rediscovery of their African identity, is celebrated. I have participated in this mass and it was a wondrous occasion.

The liturgy takes place outdoors, preferably in a special place, such as the woods where initiation takes place. A bamboo hedge is decorated with triangles and lozenges. At the head of the procession two sisters spread flowers along the pathway and all around the area of celebration. The altar is the trunk of a large tree on which is placed a leopard skin. Beside the altar, a wood fire is lighted.

After the procession arrives before the *kachisi* (a special place of initiation), the celebrant opens the door with a cross and goes in first, followed by the faithful. He bows at the altar, goes round it, and presents the theme of the celebration. He invites the faithful to ask God for mercy. This prayer for God's mercy introduces to the ritual exchange of a gesture of peace, during which every sister comes to the altar and exchanges the greeting of peace with the celebrant and goes back to exchange greetings with others.

Then the Gloria is sung and a brief moment of silence is observed before the readings. All scriptural readings are sung. Preaching and proclamation of the Christian faith take place, followed by the offerings. The offering ceremony is a special one. Sisters bring to the altar different things representing the products of their work, such as fruits, eggs, salads, flour, art works, and so forth. The preface and eucharistic prayer are sung in the African way of dialog between the celebrant and the faithful. After the moment of consecration, one or two sisters lie down before the altar and creep toward the altar, shouting praises to God; their words are repeated by all the assembly. Most of the time the celebrant and the faithful are sitting down, which is the usual position during all important gatherings in Africa.

Analyzing These Orders of Worship

The first pattern that inspires these African eucharist celebrations is the gathering of the people around their chief. When a chief organizes a consultation about any problem, he sends a herald through the villages, preferably in the night, when people are ready to sleep. The herald shouts,

"Tomorrow all the rulers of families and clans are wanted by the chief. No one is to go to farms. At the sound of the drum, everyone is expected to be at the chief's palace."

In the morning, when the people gather, a member of the chief's court welcomes them and invites them to sit down. They will talk until the chief—wearing his chieftaincy attire—comes out. The people stand up to greet him. The chief greets the people and sits down. The people do the same. The chief begins by asking the news from the various clans. There is the process of African "palaver," and then silence is required. The chief explains the main problem of the meeting. The people discuss or debate solutions proposed, and everyone has the opportunity to give an idea or opinion until the assembly arrives at consensus. The last word is given to the chief, who ratifies the result he discerns as the consensus of the assembly.

While this is going on, drink and food are made ready. A meal is always served and taken, as the expression and instrument of the communion and solidarity. No meeting at the chief's palace can be resolved without eating and drinking, because the chief is considered as a provider of his people. If the problem concerned is severe and necessitates a sacrifice to the ancestors, the assembly ends by going to the shrine or hut of the ancestors. A goat will be immolated and the assembly returns to await the preparation of the meat. Before eating they return to the knoll. The chief takes a piece of meat with a bit of dough or flour and leaves it at the doorstep of the hut of the ancestors or at the foot of the ancestors' tree. He says, "We are here because . . . [whereupon he states the reason for the assembly]. Here is the goat [or chicken] that we consecrate to you, our ancestors. Help us." He leaves the symbolic offering and retires. And then the meal is eaten.

Rites of reconciliation are also always accompanied by a meal. A meeting is called by the eldest member. When all are assembled, a discussion takes place concerning what has happened. Individuals confess their roles, admit their faults, in particular those most upset discuss their sense of being offended and the way in which they have harbored resentment. Those present give counsel and finally have the belligerents drink from the same cup. Often the cup is filled with water in which an herb has been stirred and turned symbolizing the dissolution of sin and false words. After they drink it, an animal is immolated, most often a chicken given by the guilty person. The meat is shared among all of the members of the clan and a piece of the meat is reserved for the angered ancestor. The meat is offered with dough or flour, in the same manner as the previous rite described.

In my opinion, in these two orders of worship, that of the assembly around a chief and of a sacrificial meal in honor of the memory of an ancestor or the reparation of a conflict, the desire to obtain assistance from above is apparent. In a celebration organized in 1969 by the Association of Episcopal Conferences of East Africa (AMECEA) a text introducing communion reads:

> Here is your food [they are addressing God]
> Here is your drink
> All of this is yours, before it is ours. . . .
> We celebrate a feast,
> But it is a feast of thanksgiving,
> We thank God.
> O God, we and our ancestors
> The fathers of our people
> We thank you and we rejoice.
> This food, we will eat it in Your honor.
> This drink, we will drink it in Your honor.

This structure resembles the words said by the elder in his offering to the ancestors according to the ancient traditions. We can also add that the invocation of the ancestors at the beginning of the mass within the larger grouping of the saints corresponds without doubt to the schema of sacrifices and communal meals.

The word always comes first within traditional African ritual, as it does in Christian worship. Words give meaning to gestures, and this is true in all human rites. Symbols must not only be surrounded by words but with representations that also channel meaning. The word precedes Christian eucharist as an inheritance from the Jewish usage in the synagogue, where the reading of the Law and the Prophets was placed at the beginning of the liturgy. In Africa it is certainly true that the word takes a place of honor. The mass of Cameroon highlights this by beginning with a consecration of the word of God by blessing of a book.

One of the originalities of the liturgy of Ndzon-Mellen is that the Gloria is placed after the consecration. We should note that even in the Roman liturgy the Gloria was not always fixed in its present place and that it appears quite late. It is a song of praise that can be replaced by another. But to place it after the consecration makes one think that it is at the consecration that God descends to the altar. This idea is not completely correct, because God is present in the whole of the eucharistic prayer. The transformation of bread and wine into the body and blood of Christ does not happen only at the consecration but in the unity of the eucharistic prayer.

Another African innovation is the placement of the penitential act after the word and homily or the prophecy. This can be justified because it is the word of God that is revealed to us in the expectation of conversion. The kiss of peace also follows the penitential act. This provides the perspective that reconciliation comes as the fruit of pardon, which serves to emphasize the communal and ecclesial dimension of God's pardon of

everyone. Its place before the offering and immediately after the penitential rite is closer to the gospel portrayal of this sentiment in Matthew
5:23-24, which says, "When you are offering your gift at the altar, if you
remember that your brother or sister has something against you, leave
your gift there before the altar and go; first be reconciled to your brother
or sister, and then come and offer your gift."

In certain orders of worship the Our Father is moved to the end of the
celebration. In the Roman rite this prayer is interpreted as preparatory
for communion, perhaps alluding to the connection of this phrase "give
us this day our daily bread." But this petition does not regard food alone,
nor does it signify exclusively the eucharist. "Our daily bread" is far
more. It is God's word that nourishes and God's grace that sustains our
life. One's labor in the soil to produce fruit is also offered for blessing.
Protestant and Eastern rite liturgies have moved the Our Father to different places in their celebrations. It seems to me that placing it at the
end of the liturgy regains the original significance of the prayer in the
gospels.

One further element will be discussed, integrating the ancestors in the
eucharistic prayer in Cijiba.

A New Language in Prayer

A new development can be seen in the originality of formal prayer in
African eucharist celebrations. To better see these developments in rela-
tion to the prayers of the Roman Missal let us take for example the Luba
Missal. Here we see the difference in the invocation of God, on the one
hand in the language of the ancestral tradition of the Bantu of South
Africa, and on the other hand the corresponding prayer in the Roman
Missal. The example is taken from the offertory prayer for the Fourth
Sunday in Ordinary Time.

Roman Missal	*Luba Missal*
Altaribus tuis, Domine,	Maweja of Cyame, storm who
munera nostrae	strips those who wear kente
servitutis inferimus,	cloths, wind who whirls the
quae, placatus assumens,	grass, here is our gift.
sacramentum nostrae redemptionis	But where is yours?
efficias.	We await you, now and in the
	days to come, with your Son,
	our Savior, who lives and
	reigns with you and the Holy Spirit.

In the traditional religion of the Bantus one finds the invocation of
God as the "Maweja son of Cyame" reinforcing a note of tenderness and
like "the wind who whirls the grass" it marks his omnipotence and om-

nipresence. Let us also note this ancient tradition of offering firstfruits: "Here is your part, where is ours?" The Luba Missal has united these two traditions and concludes with a Christian affirmation that Godself is the Supreme gift, the true good of humanity: "We await you."

Many other prayers in this missal borrow from the Bantu traditional titles such as *chief* or *ancestor* or expressions of God's omnipotence or God's ubiquity.[13]

NEW EUCHARISTIC PRAYERS

The African has a unique way to praise God and give thanks, to seek intercession and to "remember." The prayers we have already discussed give evidence of the way in which the people of Africa express their faith. "To praise God for all his gifts, crowned with salvation made possible by Jesus Christ," remains the imperative. This section will focus particularly on the preface of the eucharistic service.

The preface is a prayer of praise addressed to the Father, recalling God's awesome power and beneficence. That graciousness culminates in the offering of salvation in Jesus Christ. Most prefaces in African rites follow this pattern.[14] Some, however, take titles applied generally to God ("the Father") and apply them to Jesus Christ.[15] For example, in the preface to the mass on Cijibian Holy Thursday, the congregation repeats, "Jesus, Jesus, you are the Holy One." Is this a distortion of the proper theological function of the preface? Further reading of this same preface does reveal prayers directed to God the Father, and so I believe a balance is maintained. Furthermore, the Christian tradition does contain prayers addressed directly to Christ during the celebration of the eucharist. One can see a similar movement *ad Christum* ("toward Christ") when the *Agnus Dei* takes place in the Roman mass in the seventh century, and more than one preface is addressed *ad Christum* in the ancient *Gelasian Sacramentary*.[16] In addition, Alcuin's preface in the votive mass *ad postulandas lacrimas* (literally, "for seeking tears") ends with *Christus Salvator noster quem laudat* ("Christ our Savior, whom he praises").[17]

The following is a sampling of African eucharistic prayers. Included are a preface, an intercession, an *epiclesis*, the words of institution, a remembrance of the living and the dead, and a doxology. We see emphasized in these prayers the importance of life, the presence of the ancestors, and the union of God and humanity as a pact of brotherhood, as well as many other images.

Eucharistic Prayer of Kenya[18]

(In all the following prayers, C means Celebrant; All means all the faithful.)

The following is based on a Kikuyu prayer.

C: O Father, Great Ancestor, we lack adequate words to thank you, but we are certain that in your great wisdom you can see how much we appreciate your glorious gifts. O Father, when we contemplate your grandeur, we are seized with fear. O Great Ancestor, master of things on earth and in heaven, we are your soldiers, ready to act according to your wishes. Hear us, God of all ages, hear us, ancient God, who has ears. Look at us, God of all ages. Look at us, ancient God, who has eyes. Receive us, ancient God, who has hands.

The following is based on a Kikuyu prayer.

C: O Great Ancestor, who lives on the brilliant mountains, your blessing permits the increase of our properties; your anger, their destruction. We implore you, and in this we are in harmony with the spirits of our ancestors. We ask you to send us the Spirit of life *(the following is said with hands extended)* to bless and sanctify these offerings, that they may become for us the Body and the Blood of Jesus our brother and your son. On the night of his Passion, he gave thanks for the bread, which he held in his hands. This bread he divided among his friends, saying: You all, take this and eat it. It is my Body, which will be given up for you.

All: Amen. We believe that this is truly your Body.

C: And then he shared the drink with them saying: Take this and drink it. It is my Blood, the Blood of the pact of brotherhood, which begins today and will last forever. This Blood will be poured out for you, and for all men so that they may be relieved of their sins. Do this and remember me.

All: Amen. We believe that this is truly your Blood.

C: Let us proclaim the Mystery of Faith.

The following is based on a Luyia prayer.

All: O Sun of Justice, you raise yourself in the east by the command and power of God. Take away our sins. Take us by this mystery into your death and resurrection just as the sun sets and rises anew.

The following is based on a Meru prayer.

C: Owner of all things, we offer you this cup in memory of your Son. We ask life from you. Make us a healthy people, without illness. May we have infants in good health. And for women who suffer because they are sterile, heal them so that they may see their own children. Give our fathers and mothers and our ancestors who are with you a good life.

The following is based on a Kikuyu prayer.

C: Make our elders joyful and wise, and may they speak in one voice.

All: Glory to God. May peace be with us!

C: May the people enjoy peace and communion, with Mary our great Mother and all the saints.

All: Glory to God. May peace be with us!

C: May our supreme bishop John Paul and our bishop—N.—enjoy wisdom and life.

All: Glory to God. May peace be with us!

C: May the people, the flocks, and the fields prosper.

All: Glory to God. May peace be with us!

The following is based on a Kikuyu prayer.

All: O Father, your power is the greatest of all powers.

O Son, under your direction we have nothing to fear.

O Spirit, under your protection there is nothing that we cannot conquer. Amen.

The following is a prayer of the Igbo.

C: Osebulu (Lord), Chukwu (God), the almighty, we praise you! Creator of the world, Chi (God), the master of life, we praise you! Our Father, Father of our ancestors, we are gathered to praise you and to thank you with our sacrifice. Your children are before you, offering you thanks, praising you, and rejoicing in you; because you are our life; because you direct and protect each one of us; because you give us life and make us grow in the world. Your power and glory are evident in the heavens and on earth. The sun, the moon, and the stars that fill the sky proclaim your glory. This beautiful earth on which we live is the work of your hands. The food, fruit of the land, which gives us life, is your blessing.

All: Father, full of glory and majesty, we praise you. Chi, master of life, our guide, we praise you!

C: Father, full of glory and majesty, we recognize that we are not worthy to assemble before you. Our sins bring evil into the world. But your love and forgiveness encircle us. You have made your will known among us. You guided our ancestors and all humanity and taught them your way, because you wish that the entire world know your beauty. Oh, that the whole world be made aware of the fullness of life in you.

All: We thank you, Lord, the guide of our fathers! Your bounty on our behalf is without limit! Your love for us is without limit!

C: Chukwu (God), our creator, we stand before you in joy, praising
        you and glorifying you for the most beautiful action that you have
        done in this world. You sent us your own beloved son, and it is he
        who has accomplished your promises to the sons of man, he showed
        us your love and your bountifulness and made us understand that
        you are Chi (God), our Savior. He is close to you, our eyes and our
        ears. He has shown us how to see you, how to hear you, how to
        adore you, so that we may have the fullness of life.

All: We thank you, Father. We thank you for our Savior Jesus Christ!

C: When he had finished the work you had sent him to do, when he
        was ready to give his life for us, the night before his Passion, while
        they were eating, he took bread, praised you, and gave it to the
        disciples saying: Take this, all of you, and eat it. It is my body! The
        sacrificial victim for you! At the end of the feast, he took the cup of
        blessing, thanked you, and praised you for all of your admirable
        works and gave it to his disciples saying: Take this, all of you and
        drink, it is my blood! The seal of the Covenant, it washes away
        sins. It binds me to you and to all people, as part of the eternal
        family of God. Do this in memory of me!

C: Father, we proclaim the death of Christ!

All: His death on the cross!

C: We jump for joy because of his resurrection!

All: His wondrous resurrection!

C: We wait for his return on the last day!

All: For we will enter the celebration of eternal life!

C: In your love and bounty, look upon this sacrifice. Accept it because
        of Christ your son and our brother. Accept it because of your be-
        nevolence toward us. Send us your Spirit, the Spirit of your son,
        the spirit of life, the one who teaches the believers, the guide of our
        fathers, who rests upon this sacrifice that we may be filled with life
        and truth that this banquet of the body and blood of Christ will
        keep us in your family. Father, bless this family, your family, which
        you have sanctified in the blood of Christ.

All: Father, hear our voice.

C: Remember our brothers and sisters, our infants, who are not yet in
        this new family. In the light of your spirit, illuminate them so that
        they may see in Christ the fulfillment of the prayers of our ances-
        tors.

All: Father, hear our voice.

C: Be the strength of those you have chosen to be guides of your church.
        Give them wisdom and understanding.

All: Father, hear our voice.

C: Bless all of the countries of the world. Give them love, unity, and peace.

All: Father, hear our voice.

C: Bless this beautiful earth on which we live. Give it an abundance of inhabitants and food.

All: Father, hear our voice.

C: Cure the sick, console those who suffer, give to eat those who are hungry.

All: Father, hear our voice.

C: Have pity on our brothers and our sisters who have died, give them the fullness of life.

All: Father, hear our voice.

C: Unite us with all of your people, in particular with our ancestors who followed your will; with Mary, the mother of your son, Jesus; with the apostles; with all who have done what is pleasing to you.

All: Father, hear our voice.

C: We join together our voices to theirs in praising you, in thanking you, in imploring you, Holy Father, through Christ your son in the Spirit of life, so that our prayer will be received by you; so that we may enter the life that has no end.

All: Amen.

The following is a preface used in Congo (Zaire).

C: Truly, Lord, it is right that we give you thanks, that we glorify you, our God; you, our Father; you, the almighty; you, the sun at which we cannot stare; you, who are sight itself; you, the master of all people; you, the master of life; you, the master of all things; we praise you. We give you thanks through your Son, Jesus Christ, our mediator.

All: Amen. He is the only mediator.

C: Holy Father, we praise you through your Son, Jesus Christ, our mediator. He is your word, which gives life. Through him you created the heavens and the earth. Through him you created the rivers of the world, the streams, the brooks, the lakes, and all the fish that live in them. Through him you made the stars, the birds of the sky, the forests, the plains, the savanna, the mountains, and all the animals that live in them. Through him you created all things seen and unseen.

All: Amen. Through him you created all things.

C: You made him master of all things; you sent him among us so that he could become our redeemer and our savior. He is God become human. Through the Holy Spirit, he took flesh through the Virgin Mary. This we believe.

All: Amen. This we believe.

C: You sent him to assemble all peoples, so that they would become one people. He obeyed. He died on the cross. He conquered death. He rose from the dead. Can he die again?

All: No. He rose from the dead. He conquered death forever.

C: That is why, with all the angels with all the saints, with all of the dead who are near to you, we say (or sing): You are holy.

All: Holy, Holy, Holy.

The following are examples of intercessions used in Uganda and are based on a Karimojong prayer.

C: God is with us, no?

All: He is with us.

C: God will always be with us, no?

All: He will always be with us.

C: Through trials and suffering.

All: He is here.

C: With our holy father the pope, John Paul, and our bishop (N.)

All: He is near.

The following is a doxology used in Uganda.

C: With Mary our Mother and all the friends of his son.

All: He is near.

C: God has heard.

All: He has heard through Christ, in the Spirit. He has heard. Amen.

The following doxology comes from the Congolese (Zairian) mass and is sung.

C: Lord, let us glorify your name.

All: Amen.

C: Your name.

All: Amen.

C: So honorable.

All: Amen.

C: Father,

All: Amen.

C: Son,

All: Amen.

C: Holy Spirit,

All: Amen.

C: Let us glorify your name.

All: Amen.

C: Today,

All: Amen.

C: Tomorrow,

All: Amen.

C: Forever and ever,

All: Amen.

Ancestors in the Eucharist

The prayers presented in the previous section contain references to the ancestors. The fact that the ancestors are mentioned in the eucharistic prayer reveals a fundamental African conception of the structure of the world and of human life. What is the place of ancestors in the life of a Christian black African? What role do the ancestors play in the economy of salvation through Jesus Christ? If they have an important and valid place in daily life, one cannot have a Christian eucharist in Africa without including them. This section addresses some fundamental questions related to the presence of the ancestors in Black African prayer.

Vision of the World and of Life

At the end of a series of invocations of the saints in the Congolese (Zairian) entrance rite, the following invocation is made: "And you, our ancestors, be with us, you who have served God with a right conscience, be with us. Here is our prayer, be with us all, we who celebrate the mass at this moment."

By way of comparison, let us look for a moment at the African celebration in Paris at a 1981 meeting of African and Western theologians. The mass begins with an invocation of the African ancestors: "Oh, you ancestors of Zimbabwe, you who cultivated the banks of the Orange and Zambese, you who have hunted the buffalo and antelope in the savannas of Twana and Shoto, you who have brought into the world the San, the Khoi, the Zulu. . . . Be with us." The liturgical celebration continues with the citation of different peoples of Black Africa and concludes invoking Christian ancestors: "And you, our ancestors in the faith, you who in Ethiopia, North Africa, and Uganda have died in faith as followers of

Christ, you Augustine, Lwanga and his companions, European and American missionaries who died in our African land, be with us."

These two texts constitute two very different ways of invoking the ancestors. In the first text, the invocation of the ancestors is placed after the invocation of the saints. This is a perspective that recalls the memory of the ancestors through the channel of the "righteous" who have died and been saved through Christ, even though they would not have encountered Christ himself, who came after them.[19] This same perspective can be found in the other text of African eucharistic prayers. For example, the Kenyan prayer calls God the "Great Elder," signaling a communion with the ancestors during the mass: "And in this we are in harmony with the spirits of our ancestors." A Nigerian prayer also mentions the ancestors as those who had been guided as children of God, as those who did the will of God.

In the second text the ancestors are invoked before the saints. In this way the preoccupation is on the communion in life between parents and children, which must be in place prior to any important action. The saints are added after the ancestors to underscore the fact that those who are beyond "the clan" form part of the union of members as well, thanks to the new source of communion, that is, the blood of Christ. But this new source for the communion in life between members does not sublimate the original resource, that of ancestral mediation.

Black Africans, the Bantu in particular, have a unified view of life, as we have said above. The world is a whole with God at the summit, the ancestors and benevolent spirits follow, then malevolent spirits and the "strong" of this world, and finally, humans as terrestrial beings. The common denominator that binds these beings is life. God is the unique source of the life in which all participate. Participation in "life" takes place in different degrees, which permits an interdependence according to levels of being and affinity.[20] There is certainly an "above" and "below," but they co-penetrate rather than exist separately. That is to say, they are continually present to one another. The one is transcendent and the other immanent. The interdependence of the members of a Bantu clan is such that an individual receives life through the ancestors and is unthinkable apart from them. As the individual grows in life, communion with the ancestors intensifies and this intensification has an impact on the other members of the clan.

The ancestors are the first who received the force of life from God. They represent the highest level of being beneath God in the pyramid of beings. But they remain human. Having passed through death, they are more powerful than living persons, enjoying the capacity to exercise the force of life. They can increase or diminish the force of life on earth. In their life's journey they see God and God's subjects. But it is not simply through death that one joins the ranks of the ancestors. One must have lived a good life, that is to say a virtuous life. The tradition gives the following criteria for an ancestor:

- to have followed the laws; not to have been found guilty of theft or debauchery; not to have been angry or quarrelsome; not to have been tempted by sorcery; to have been an agent of communion among people.
- to have had a descendant, since the life received must be communicated; the ancestor may not be a barrier to life, which would be the case without descendants, for how could one be a sign or play a role in the mediation of life without giving the life to others, without begetting?
- to have died well, which means first of all to have died a "natural" death; that is to say, to have lived many years, to have transmitted one's message to one's family, and to have been buried.

The ancestors are therefore mediators (through the power of the Supreme Being, because everything comes from God) in helping the people to be fertile, healthy, and prosperous. Their mode of action is rooted in the family lineage and consanguinity. Blood is the pathway for the interaction of life's forces. Their role as mediators is reinforced in the ordinary life of the Bantu people, especially in the ritual communal meals when the family gathers around the ancestral tree. Before drinking, they pour a small amount onto the ground. This is a sign of deference and acknowledgment that ancestors continue to participate in their lives. If someone accidentally sneezes, he or she will utter the name of an ancestor, as if to say, "Be with me in what happens."

The compatibility and vitality of this communion with the ancestors and Christian tradition may be illustrated by several examples. A religious sister from Zaire was considered to be an "instigator of revolt" among the young sisters because she challenged a conservative priest over the issue of religious habits. This traditionalist priest was ignoring the reforms of the Second Vatican Council and insisting that the sisters remain in their Western habits. In addition, he considered African clothing to be "like a prostitute's garments." Her expulsion from the congregation was decided upon. But the night before it occurred, she confided in her dead father, saying, "You, my father, you know my sincerity in bringing the others to challenge this old goat who has led us to a chasm. Do something up there. Intervene in this affair!" Before the meeting could take place, the priest had a visit from his superior, and his decision was reversed.

Several years later, on the day she was to travel to Brussels, the same sister had her purse stolen. In it was her passport, Belgian currency, letters of introduction, and her airplane ticket. She started to cry but also to have thoughts of her father. She said, "Papa, don't sleep." She retraced her steps, telling everyone that her purse had been stolen. Two hours later, when she returned in a car with other sisters to the place it had been taken, they spotted a crowd and drove over to it. One of the men called out to them, "My sisters, a religious sister has been robbed. The picture on her passport and her identity card show that she is a nun. Can you bring this purse to the head of the mission in the hopes that you will be able to find her?" And they told him right away who she was.

An African priest, while he was a student in France, tried to have one of his sisters, who was very ill, come for treatment. He tried many ways to make the arrangements, but each time he failed. One night he thought intensely of his dead mother and asked her to do something. The following morning he went to see a French priest. In a moment the priest signed a document that proved to be the key to solving the problem.

These examples indicate the possibility of coexistence, where the commitment to Christianity obvious in the lives of these individuals did not prevent them from relying on traditional forms of prayer to ancestors in times of crisis. We should prevent "learned" people from ridiculing or minimizing the influence of the ancestors.

God and the Ancestors

When one examines traditional prayers, one finds no conflict between God and the ancestors in traditional religion. The following is one example from traditional prayer:

> My father, my ancestor, you who are in the region of this world, you, with God and the earth, it is you who speak. As for me, I see nothing anywhere. Take and receive this [chicken] feather and bring it to the Being whom you know, because of your closeness, so that peace may come upon me.[21]

In this example the ancestor-father's role as mediator is clear. The ancestors are closer to the source of favors. They are well placed to see both human and divine plans. In addition, one sees that in the ritual of sacrifice of a chicken or a goat to the ancestor, God is the addressee of the rite.

> God of the heavens, Lord, give me force and life, so that I may be strong. . . . Zira [an ancestor], it is true. God of the sky, . . . receive this white cock and give it to grandfather; Zira, it is the white cock, it is yours I offer. . . . Protect your grandson and granddaughters. . . . Look at me, protect me, night and day. . . . Protect me at the market, protect my wife while she is preparing, let there always be food in this house.[22]

In African Christianity—at least in principle—there is no conflict between invoking ancestors and respecting the ontological uniqueness of

God because the ancestors are never considered the ultimate recourse. That role remains with God. If the role of the ancestors were ever considered to be absolute, then invoking them could be the sin of idolatry. Even in traditional Bantu religion that would be considered a misrepresentation and an error! The ancestors are allies of God. They are always at God's side doing the divine will. Because of their dedication to the will of God, they find a place alongside belief in the gospel, which is God's word expressing God's will.

Ancestors and the Saints

The exemplary life of the ancestors also plays a role today. Their example can be a model for the moral life, serving as guides to our societies, and that can indeed include Christians. Benezet Bujo presents an excellent argument that becomes a theological rehabilitation of the memory of the ancestors who have always been central to Black African culture. On the question of "outside the church there is no salvation," the present attempts to "rehabilitate" the ancestors seems to accord with the classic Catholic response that there *are* other ways to blessedness when the ordinary way is not available. Thus there is confidence that there are righteous ones who have been saved without having encountered Christ in the church. The love of God shines above all else: "Whatever is true, whatever is honorable, whatever is just, whatever is pure, whatever is pleasing, whatever is commendable, if there is any excellence and if there is anything worthy of praise, think about these things" (Phil 4:8), because we have already experienced the firstfruits of salvation in Christ.

It is true that not everything that is good, beautiful, or true in this world can serve as a symbol of salvation through Christ. The blood of a Christian who dies on the battlefield for national liberation does not function in the same way as the blood of a Christian martyred for his faith, even if both are examples worthy of emulation, even if the two count among the mediations between God and humanity. Abraham, Isaac, and Jacob, the just of the Old Testament, are numbered with Christian saints, since they counted on the promise of the Messiah and were in the line of those promises. Our African ancestors, as they practiced love of neighbor and clan, were not waiting for a messiah. But this does not exclude them from being objects of divine solicitude. It is not their fault that they did not encounter Christ. I am certain that God has reserved a comfortable place for them somewhere.

In ordinary Christian experience a piety revolving around the saints included reverence for those who were not martyrs. In the third and fourth centuries, for example, Romans had the habit of going to the tombs of their dead and presenting them gifts. There they would eat a meal, with the understanding that their dead family members were able to share the meal with them. Christians followed this practice too, not only in memory of their individual families but also to remember the heroes of the faith, the martyrs.[23] St. Augustine did not condemn such practices.[24] Instead, he tried to turn them into acts of beneficence, inviting the poor and distributing offerings, and into moments of prayer for the deceased.[25]

Christians went to the tombs of martyrs in the third and fourth centuries, not simply to pray but to steep themselves in the spiritual force of the martyr. This was called *incubation*. All these practices could be perceived as ambiguous, but they were supported by a Christian rationale that held that the church was fortified by the blood of the martyrs and that the lives of the saints helped to support the faithful who continue to struggle below. The cult of saints was placed on this theological basis. Nonetheless, actual approval was given only *after* these practices were already in place in the life of the ordinary people.

Beginning with martyrs, the cult of saints slowly spread to include confessors, monks, pastors of the church, and finally to all who had given eloquent witness to the love of Christ in a life dedicated to God and to the Kingdom. The cult typically developed around places that had been identified in some way by the saint's example of faith. Sometimes the cult overflowed beyond the special place because of the importance of the individual in the faith of the church. This is true, for example, in the case of the Virgin Mary, the Apostles, and Saint Michael. Sometimes elements of the biography of saints led to devotion to an individual. The example of St. Anthony of Padua, to whom many turn if they lose an object, is famous. Some pray to St. Christopher if journeying across a dangerous river. Many churches eventually erected statues of the saints in a place where devotees could come to light candles as they prayed. Similarly, plaques describing miracles attributed to different saints were put up.

Looking on these Western practices from the perspective of Black African experience, the cult of saints makes Africans think of their veneration of and turning toward ancestors for help. There are numerous analogies. Ancestors continue to support members of the family alive on earth, just as saints support the family of Christians through their prayers and merits. Ancestors are at a key juncture in communion of life and their descendants, in somewhat the same way as the life of Christ is the link between the Christians on earth and the saints. Ancestors receive their power from the Supreme Being, just as the saints were moved by the power of Christ. Ancestors provide an example to follow, just as the saints do for Christians.

But certain irreducible differences between the two practices and notions remain, even if they are not in fact in direct and serious conflict. These differences reside essentially in the core aspect that saints are models of perseverance in faith in Jesus Christ, witnesses of a total love that entails giving one's life for Jesus Christ. This for Christians is the highest human good. Christian saints are the witnesses of the fulfillment and joy that one achieves in attachment to Jesus Christ. Neither having known or lived the faith in Jesus Christ, our African ancestors cannot play this role as witnesses. Neither can their valor be exemplary because of Christian origins. Therefore, our African ancestors do not need the designation "saints" to merit our veneration. They are venerable as they are, that is to say, as founders of our societies, peacemakers among human beings, intermediaries between us and the Supreme Being, as forces present in our everyday life. The ancestors also remain in need of us, that is to say, according to traditional beliefs they need descendants who continue the growth of life begun in them. Therefore, they are in need of Jesus Christ, for they continue to journey with us in a special way. This does not impede their role as intermediaries.

Mediations by the Ancestors and the Mediation of Christ

Christ is the mediator between God and humanity. Does this mean that there is no need for other mediators? Does this mean that God could not turn to another human being to save someone? Does this mean that someone can no longer, through mortification and prayers, obtain grace for another? One should ask whether recognizing the universal mediation of Christ must annul other mediations provided Christ's is recognized as supreme. The mediation of Christ makes possible all other mediations.

The mediation of Christ is universal and ultimate. It achieves its fullness in the cross and the glorification. The mediation of the ancestors is limited to their descendants and does not achieve the plenitude of the Kingdom of God. Its efficacy is not comprehensible except within the grace of Christ, who reveals the infinite love of God. Before the revelation of Christ, our ancestors were a sign of the nearness of God, of the love of God. They remained so after this revelation, even if a more astonishing sign has been given in the incarnation of God himself.

The important principle involved here is whether it is true that Christ did not come to supplant all other signs of God's love that exist throughout creation. In the interpretation we are advancing, he did not come to erase the signs of the presence of God in the world that our ancestors recognized, signs that comprise, in effect, the "footprints" of the one who had fashioned the universe. Rather, his coming confirmed these signs, sealed them. Christ effectively confirmed that God intervenes in the world through diverse mediations, and that in this way he presents himself as the supreme mediator, assuming headship over all mediations without destroying them.

To say that Christ is the unique priest and intercessor is not to deny the usefulness to human existence of other priests and intercessors. Rather, it affirms that one must understand them as expressing Christ's own priesthood and his role as intercessor. Christ as the unique priest does not sublimate human mediations; rather, they are accomplished through him.

In this light one can say then that the mediation exercised by the ancestors is accomplished through the mediation of Christ. We conclude that Africans may continue to turn to their ancestors to ask spiritual and material graces of them, as long as these appeals are understood as subordinate to Christ, who alone is our salvation. Are there dangers? Certainly. All believers, for instance, are tempted to desire God's favors more than to desire God. Corporal and spiritual at the same time, Christians everywhere need to touch the wounds of the resurrected Jesus and to say with Thomas, "my lord and my savior," and, "truly this was the son of God." By invoking our African ancestors, we proclaim the divine goodness manifested in these mediations and we prepare ourselves to comprehend the mediation of the Son of God, the sublime and total manifestation of God's goodness. To invoke my ancestors is also to recognize the communion of life that continues into the hereafter and continues to affect my being. It should lead to believing that my dedication to Christ is not an individual affair that merely passes. It is held deep within the foundation of my being in relation to my entire community. A Muntu Christian cannot adhere totally and with the fullness of his being to Christ without also joining that faith to roots that continue to nourish the buds of the trunk of the tree. The invocation of the ancestors, understood properly, simply proclaims in a clearer way the truth that Christ is the essence and the summit of *all* life, the alpha and the omega of *all* action.

Forms of Integration

One can conclude from the discussion above that—since the eucharist is a high point in the exchange of life's essence and force—Bantu Christians could not conceive of celebrating the eucharist without including the ancestors. Many forms of integrating the ancestors in the sacramental life of the Christian church have developed over time.

The most frequent form and the most widespread in Black Africa is the invocation. One invites the ancestors to participate in the prayer, in the action that is about to take place: "Be with us, make yourself present in what is happening at this moment." This "be with" is not in the sense of "stay next to me." Nor is it in the Heideggerian sense of "coexist with." In Bantu languages the importance accorded to the category "be with" is one where there is no verb "to have" or "to possess." These are civilizations that are fundamentally relational, where there is a clear sense of community and solidarity. When you are truly with another, you commune with his or her being, and you take into consideration what the person holds in his or her heart. You want what he or she wants. If you could, you would give it to the person.

To invoke the ancestors by saying within the eucharist celebration "be with me" reveals that there is a movement toward communion, toward solidarity and harmony in the project of life inaugurated by Christ and transmitted through the eucharist. This also reveals that one continues to share with the ancestors all the ultimate growth of life. Also, in this ritual action where life is in play, one must invoke the ancestors and make them participate. It is in this way that each ritual action where one eats and drinks can be a meal shared with the ancestors. One may make a simple invocation if there is nothing to drink or eat during the rite.

In all of the ancient ceremonies where the ancestors were asked to share a meal or an offering of an animal or another gift such as flour or beer, one did not pour out on the ground all the flour, beer, or meat. Rather, one laid down a morsel, a small bit, which was symbolic of the entire gift. Today it is difficult for people who live in cities to find a place for sacrifices and offerings. In this situation they often pour a little palm wine or beer on the ground and accompany that act with a series of appropriate invocations.[26] During official receptions in the Democratic Republic of Congo between 1970 and 1996, one poured a taste of whatever drink was being consumed into a small pot filled with ashes intended for the communion with ancestors.

If the eucharist is a meal, a meal of life, then one can only integrate the ancestors by making a link between them and the gifts of the meal of the Lord. A branch from a tree of the ancestors is placed in a great vase painted white (the color of the ancestors) and placed in front of the altar at the beginning of the celebration. After the song "Lamb of God," during which the bread is broken, two acolytes lift the vase and present it to the assembly. The commentator explains:

> The tree that you see before you recalls our ancestors; its encounter with Christ bears for us inestimable gifts; it is in these gifts that we want to solidify our communion with our ancestors; the sacrifice of Christ is the definitive cement of our communion in life.

The priest takes the host, dips it in the wine, and moves toward the vase saying:

> You, our ancestors, Jesus, whom we call the Christ, has come among us with a new pledge. His offering exceeds everything that we have thus far offered to God, all that we have offered you. We participate in his sacrifice to flourish and be saved. Be with us. We join with you so that you also may attain the fullness of life in the new heaven.

He places the host on the paten and places the paten at the foot of the tree. The acolytes return the vase to the foot of the altar and take their places. The priest receives communion and the faithful after him. After the purification of the chalice, the host will be consumed by the priest as the newest elder.

Is there confusion with that offering to the ancestors? It seems not. The host is not abandoned at the foot of the tree. We bring the ancestors to the foot of the altar of the Lord, as the place for their fulfillment. In 1968 an African priest proposed that the tree of the ancestors be drawn on the furniture of the choir.[27] When we look further we read:

> Our small hut for the spirits must be in our church. . . . One must draw a great tree for the spirits on the altar where we celebrate the mass. In this way, when we enter the church, we will think of our dead ancestors and we will honor their spirit.[28]

To put the host at the foot of the tree, which is at the base of the altar, is a new framework and changes the orientation of the traditional symbol. The priest, as president of the new assembly and the new elder of the Christian family, comes to consume the host. In the traditional ceremony the offering must stay in place, to be eaten by an animal or insects. Here it is quite different. The elder consumes it. In this we find a new development in African thinking as it encounters Christian worship.

There is also another rite, signifying the participation of ancestors. The priest, carrying a vase of water, approaches an earthenware jar in which the tree is planted. He blesses the water by putting a cross of Jesus into the water and saying:

> You, our ancestors, we do not forget you in the path that we now take with Jesus, who has brought us a new promise; may this water, which has been consecrated by the cross of Jesus and his glorification, make you grow in heaven and draw you into communion with the fullness of time that we know in Jesus Christ. Be with us.

He then pours out the water around the tree and returns to the altar for communion.

These are examples of the integration of the ancestors into Christian liturgy. It seems, if the reader agrees with our discussion, that their presence in a eucharistic celebration may be appropriate and enhance both the African Christian's self-understanding and grasp of the Christian tradition.

.

CELEBRATING THE EUCHARIST
WITH AFRICAN FOOD AND DRINK

Father René Jaouen, an Oblate of Mary Immaculate and missionary in Africa, has written a book about the case for using an African cereal (mil) in North Cameroon for Christian eucharist.[29] His arguments are based on the sacred character of this cereal in Cameroon and on the anthropology of the rites and the truth of the language. I complement his argument in our discussion by drawing attention to the internal coherence of the Christian liturgy and to the theological argument from the dynamic of incarnation and of the memorial.

THE HISTORICAL ARGUMENT

The actual bread of the host and wine of our mass have changed over time. They are certainly not the same as Christ used on Holy Thursday. The Jews were Semites, originally a semi-nomadic people. They made their bread with a variety of grains, but their cultic breads, and in particular their bread of blessing, were comprised of a base of five cereals: wheat, barley, corn, millet, and oats.[30] These cereals belong to the family of rye, sorghum, and rice. At the time of Jesus the bread of daily life was made from wheat, but also of other cereals. In John 6:9 a young man brought along the route five barley loaves and two small fishes. Among their breads used in the temple, the Jews had breads of oblation, which were a part of vegetable offerings. They were placed in two rows on a dressed table before the Holy of Holies and replaced every Sabbath.[31] In particular we note breads without leaven that were eaten during the feast of Passover. Passover was primarily a rite of shepherds, nomads, and semi-nomads, very closely related to the ancient Arabs, among whom blood rites were emphasized. The Passover rite was designed to obtain fertility and prosperity for the herd. Among the Israelites the rite was historicized and took on a special meaning by its association with the miraculous intervention by God that freed them from Egyptian bondage.

In primitive celebrations an unleavened bread is present. But, it was a "bread of pain," a bread for voyagers, such as the Bedouins continue to use, because they do not have the time to wait for it to rise. This bread will take on a certain importance on the arrival to the land of Canaan, where the Israelites will find a feast of unleavened bread as the feast of firstfruits. At the harvest, new, "pure" produce was offered ("pure" because it had never been mixed with old elements, such as leaven). And since this Canaanite feast coincided with the Passover, the two were joined together into the same celebration since the Deuteronomic reforms.[32]

It is very possible that Jesus used unleavened bread, since the eucharist was instituted at Passover, according to the synoptic gospels. Unleavened bread was used for the Passover meal and during the week after Passover in certain Jewish milieux.[33] What was important for the early Christians, as far as eucharistic elements was concerned, was the "bread" and not the unleavened nature of the bread. This is clear because the faithful brought bread from their homes for the eucharist. The eucharistic context of John 6:9 confirms this. According to M. Durry, "So many of the literary documents on the eucharist bread which are represented in pictures show that the type does not deviate from the ones used for the everyday bread; Pliny the Younger speaks of an 'ordinary' meal."[34] The custom of placing various designs on the bread has also been observed. The form of an open or closed crown with a cross on the top is one example. In the fourth and fifth centuries the monogram of the Greek characters XP ("chi-rho") figures on the ovens,[35] but the bread is leavened.

It is after the ninth century that discussion begins about the necessity of using unleavened bread for the eucharist, according to Alcuin.[36] It is not until the eleventh century, however, that the rule that unleavened bread must be used was imposed in the West. The Eastern church maintains the use of leavened bread in most churches.

Red wine remains the wine most often used, probably because it symbolizes blood. Nevertheless, it is also true that red wine was the most common wine consumed during that period. The habit was kept to mix a bit of water with it, in proportions that varied from one-third water and two-thirds wine to half and half.[37] The "Aquarians" of the third century refused to celebrate the eucharist with wine, which they saw as something that corrupts the senses. Their position was condemned at the Council of Carthage in 419.

The movement toward requiring unleavened bread was led, it seems to me, by scriptural injunctions on purity. Consider, for example, in the writings of St. Paul:

> Clean out the old yeast so that you may be a new batch, as you really are unleavened. For our paschal lamb, Christ, has been sacrificed. Therefore, let us celebrate the festival, not with the old yeast, the yeast of malice and evil, but with the unleavened bread of sincerity and truth (1 Cor 5:7-8).

The separation of the eucharist from the meal itself over time further removed the symbolic meaning of a family meal and allowed the importance of realistic, wholesome bread to erode. This development was influenced by a theology that preached separation from the world and was suspicious of matter. The liturgy of the Middle Ages became more and more an epiphany of God to contemplate as a spectator.[38] It is therefore not surprising that they looked for a "perfect" host, white, pure, uncorrupted by leaven. The eucharist is no longer normal human bread, and the sacrament has been separated from daily life.

Other parts of the church did not follow this. The Syrian "Jacobites," for example, put salt and oil in the eucharist bread[39]; more and more the Orient develops an alternative theory of the symbolism of the eucharist, in favor of leaven:

> The unleavened is something dead, inanimate since the soul of the bread, the leaven, has been removed; nowhere is it written that Jesus

took the unleavened but the *bread*; the one who takes the unleavened bread remains attached to the ceremonial law of the Jews.[40]

In the East, unleavened bread could not signify "living bread," a bread of life. The popes of the fifteenth century eventually admitted the validity of both practices for the eucharist.[41] At that time the Copts and the Ethiopians used the juice of raisins, obtained through soaking dried raisins in water.[42] And in spite of the fact that this is not produced through fermentation, the Holy Office accepted their eucharist as valid on 22 July 1706.[43]

The Protestant Reformation in the sixteenth century did not attach much importance to the question of the eucharistic elements. By restoring the people to their place in the worship, and returning that place to the culture, they consecrated the use of local elements in the celebration at the same time as the use of the vernacular language.[44] Certain Protestant theologians, while remaining theoretically open-minded, in fact resist using materials other than bread and wine. One example of this is von Allmen's account of men imprisoned during the war who celebrated the Lord's supper with a bit of water and bread or simple biscuits. This he accepts. However, he repudiates the practice in India of celebrating the eucharist with rice and tea.[45] A Russian synod, sometime between 1589 and 1605, authorized cherry wine to be used for the mass.[46] This variety of historical customs brings to the discussion some authorized cases of using elements other than bread and wine in the Latin church.

In the Western Latin tradition there are cases where liturgical law has authorized a eucharistic celebration without the canonical elements of bread from wheat flour and wine from grapes. Recall, for example, the case of imprisoned priests who were permitted to celebrate with a fermented beverage such as beer.[47] Further, from the twelfth century onward, the Latin church distributed only bread to the faithful during communion, overlooking the actual events of the Last Supper, when Christ gave the cup to all who had taken the bread and said, "All of you, take this cup and drink."[48] Scholastic theology interpreted this change as acceptable because Christ was fully present in both the bread and the wine. Furthermore, communion to the sick and to infants had always been of one kind. It seems quite clear, however, that this is a significant deviation from the actual institution of the eucharist by Christ at the Last Supper.

The sixteenth century also introduced the use of a purification cloth to clean the chalice. Mundane concerns about cleaning the purificators after their use led to the widespread shift from red wine to white wine. This disregarded the symbolic representation of the blood of Christ shown by red wine. Yet the First Provincial Synod of Milan in 1565 accepted this shift.[49] Simply stated, the history of the liturgy shows clearly that the eucharist materials can change and have not always remained the same in the Christian churches. The example of such historical precedents justifies further discussion about the needs and developments in present-day African liturgies.

The theologians who oppose the use of elements besides bread and wine for the eucharist present three important arguments: (1) the historicity of Jesus Christ's act on Holy Thursday, when he used bread made from wheat flour and wine from the vine and said that they should repeat this action in memory of him; (2) the tradition of the Latin church and scholastic theology, which insists and maintains the necessity of unleavened bread and wine from the vine for the eucharist; and (3) the unity of the church, which demands that the eucharistic species be imported or these Mediterranean cereals be cultivated wherever needed.

Jesus took bread and wine so that he could celebrate with his disciples. No one thought to challenge him. He was using the accepted staple common in meals in his times. Jesus was born a Jew not because Judaism constituted a theological necessity, but because to be human meant to be situated in time and in a place. There are no universal people. A human being comes from *some* place, belongs *somewhere*, and is thus conditioned by these characteristics. God, in becoming human, embraced these constraints. That is why God chose Abraham, a people, a culture, for in the midst of these contingent situations he shared the human condition. But "Mediterranean-ness" does not therefore constitute a theological necessity for salvation and for an understanding of God's nature.

To understand the saving meal, which recalls the death and resurrection of Christ as intrinsically and theologically bound to the materiality of the elements that constituted this meal in a particular culture, is to be limited by a kind of "historicism" that overvalues contingent events. If we are to follow this kind of historicism, is it necessary to repeat the words of Jesus Christ in his own language, Aramaic? Must we celebrate within the context of a meal? Use three or four cups of blessing? Ensure that all present drink at the same moment; and that the wine may only be the red wine of Palestine? This quickly declines into a kind of taboo or fetishist thinking. The eucharist is not the sacrament of bread and wine but the sacrament of the death and resurrection of Christ. It is a memorial of the death and resurrection as a saving act, and not as a memorial of Mediterranean agriculture. The sacramental memorial of Jesus is not a paschal meal bound to Jewish liturgical customs but the gift of his life as intercession and praise.

THE THEOLOGICAL ARGUMENT

When Exodus 12 speaks of memorial, it gives to later generations that celebrate the memorial this message, "Today, God saves you." It is in this way that today we must make the memorial of the death and resurrection of Christ, in the mood of a festive, ritual meal. The meaning is undermined if we do not use the equivalent "bread" and "wine" of today. It is as if one were made to speak in Aramaic, Greek, or Latin to announce the message of the gospel to people who did not speak Aramaic, Greek, or Latin. Father Boote once wrote, "But the Eucharist is the re-enactment of the last meal of Jesus, and one will never find in the gospels the words that Jesus took a bowl of rice and a cup of tea."[50] In his opinion, the biblical origins of the liturgy oblige all of humanity to attach itself to the Jewish symbolism and then adopt it for eternity.

The pretense of renewing a liturgy without making reference to people today and to the significance of the rite for them will make the liturgy a museum where one goes to meditate on ancient artifacts or to study history, where one learns to admire its heraldry. In this way the anthropological dimension of the eucharist is eliminated and the ultimately true, fundamental meaning of the memorial simply disappears. It seems to me that the materiality of the Jewish meal is not relevant to us as Christians; rather, it was a means to transmit Christ's message. I am not obliged to be Jewish to become Christian.

In the context of the civilization of the peoples of the Bible, bread and wine are essential, culturally relevant elements for nourishment. They are, in a sense, the first and principal food of the human person. Bread is considered above all as a gift from God, for which we should pray each day to our Father in heaven according to Matthew 6:11. And that is why we translate the petition in the Lord's Prayer for "our daily bread" in our languages in words that represent food itself.[51] This is explained well in the words of a Nigerian liturgist:

> The unique transformation of the Jewish ritual by Jesus does not lie in the domain of the elements. He ate and drank like any other Jew . . . products of the land. . . . Jesus used the food items of his culture because he was establishing the Eucharist in the context of a meal. . . . This means that the question of the use of wheat or barley bread and grape-wine, is not a dogmatic but a disciplinary issue. . . . We have to celebrate the Eucharist memorial with food and drink but this food and drink do not necessarily have to be wheat bread and grape-wine.[52]

Can the transposition that we easily make for all biblical symbols not be made for a wafer of millet or for a cup of palm or banana wine?

Canon Vanneste, in the name of scholastic categories of sacramental theology, refuses Africans the right to use anything except Mediterranean bread and wine. He says that we do not know any theologian who teaches that Christ instituted the eucharist in a generic manner. Rather, in his opinion, all agree that Jesus chose to indicate the essential elements of the eucharistic rite himself and that therefore they are invariable.[53] The fragile and overly relative manner of his categories makes one smile. What does the word *generic* mean in relation to the writings of the New Testament, which relate the acts of Jesus? In "he took the bread" . . . "he took the wine," how can one establish that it was specifically leavened bread and wine from the grape? When St. Thomas spoke of baptism as a sacrament of infancy and the healing oils of the sick as the entry into death, must we take as absolutes these categories and affirm that baptism is a sacrament of the young and healing with oil a sacrament of the old?

Baptism and confirmation are part of a trilogy of rites of Christian initiation. For Vanneste, they are "generically" instituted and can change according to the needs of history and cultures. The exception, of course, is the eucharist—the summit of the sacraments! Yet as we have seen in our brief historical excursion, there have been changes in the eucharist during the first four centuries in both the East and West.

Jesus said, "The human person was not made for the Sabbath, but the Sabbath for the person." Must one tie the worship of the community that follows him to Mediterranean cultural customs and material forms for all eternity? Must one demand that the people of Africa and Asia say, "Blessed are you, God of the universe, you who give us this bread, fruit of the earth and the work of human hands," yet allow them to offer only the fruits of the Mediterranean basin? Certainly not. The God who is revealed to us in the gospels is not one who goes among the people as "Emmanuel," unpacking his "sandwich," and not eating the food of the people he is with. The God of Jesus Christ is not a God on a special diet who refuses to eat and drink what the people have.

THE ECONOMIC ARGUMENT

Liturgy is tied to life. The connection between worship and social transformation is a necessity for the authenticity of ritual. "I hate your canticles . . . if they do not bring you to love my will, to take care of the widow and the orphan, to fight for the right," said Yahweh. The last part of a book in French by L. Museka Ntumba (the English title of which would be *The African Naming of Jesus Christ*) underlines well this dimension of inculturation.[54] The question of bread and wine for the eucharist enters into such an application. How could the Lord link the Mediterranean economy in such an onerous fashion to the economies of Africa and Asia, and all based on a cultural bias? R. Jaouen makes this argument persuasively in his book *L'eucharistie du mil*.

Father Mpongo proposes that we adopt cultivation of all of the cereals of the West, including wheat, as well as grow grapevines in Africa:

> I don't see what stops black Africa from producing certain varieties of cereals hitherto unknown on our soil. We think here of millet, manioc, corn, sugarcane, and a kind of rice. It would also be a mistake to think that wheat and the grape-vine pushed up magically in the Mediterranean basin. Isn't it also obvious that black Africa has accepted to live this phenomenon of inculturation by assimilating progressively these exotic agricultural commodities?

Today more than yesterday she has engaged in an irreversible process. Not only has she allowed industrialization but she has also adopted European languages and educational systems.[55]

Eating bread as a daily staple is a luxury for an African. To import wheat flour would cost a veritable fortune, while in the West, bread costs a tiny fraction of a worker's salary. Just as the unleavened bread makes one think of a "bread of misery," so our eucharistic bread ruins the poor of the country. Conscious of this problem, the United Nations Food and Agricultural Organization launched a campaign to bake bread made from African cereals such as corn or millet, for which indigenous methods of production are already in place.

To celebrate the eucharist with millet or corn in effect sets in motion a form of economic liberation. Although Africans do import technology, languages, and educational systems, these things are useful only to the extent that they are integrated appropriately in a particular project, which itself determines its role. It seems unnecessary to continue alienating our peoples.

Will the unity of the church be endangered if different regions use their native agricultural produce? We don't think so. The reference to the death and resurrection of Christ over the local meal safeguards this unity. Father Uzukwu proposes that African regions regroup themselves around the cereals most prevalent in Africa—millet and corn—and around beverages such as palm and banana wine. (It is important not to press this suggestion absolutely, since it could conceivably lead to a new economic imperialism of one African region over another.) In principle, though, we must ask whether the eucharistic elements should not correspond to the basic elements of a local meal.

In Congo (Zaire), we have successfully carried out several experiments using fresh, grated manioc soaked in water to produce a flour of fine texture. This flour produces fine slices of bread, which last over two months if they are properly baked. We have also made corn wine that remains wholesome much longer than palm wine. It is made by mixing dry corn with a double measure of sugar and four measures of water. This mixture is left to ferment for one month then strained. It produces a milky wine with an alcoholic level of 6 to 7 percent.

Thus we draw to a close this chapter, the longest in the book. We have discussed matters from the basic principles of the eucharist to the practical questions of inculturation and its limits. Especially in the latter area, the issues are complex and controverted. We raise the issues not to promote disunity in the world church but because they are questions that will not go away, even if we do not raise them here.

4

Penance and
Reconciliation

Rites of reconciliation are among the most important rites in Black Africa, because on them depend the restoration and maintenance of life in community. In effect, our societies do not depend on technical structures but on alliances and the communion of groups. The Muntu do not fear the enemy from outside. Certainly enemies armed with guns can cause carnage. But once they are contained, the group quickly recovers. The same can be said for sorcery. As long as it remains outside, it cannot have an effect on an individual in the family. It must be introduced through the channel of a traitor within the family. "The insect that is inside the bean is the one that can destroy it with ease," is a Luba proverb.

When the enemy is within, only reconciliation can destroy its power. Consanguinity is a link through life and death. Therefore the way to end the conflict between a brother and sister who have become enemies is through reconciliation. Without it, all prosperity is illusory; all healing is merely superficial and temporary. Rites of reconciliation in our African societies are fundamental. They play both a nurturing and remedial role. They bring harmony and reestablish equilibrium.

Christian reconciliation has known a long evolution. When the Christian tradition of reconciliation arrived in Africa it encountered a profound richness within the culture. There was already present the practice of the confession of faults and of reconciliation to the community, in particular for great events in the life of the community, at childbirth, reunions, separations, disputes, and other sorts of disruptions to the equilibrium. I have already written on this subject for Western audiences.[1] But after further research and discussion with pastors and African theologians,[2] I feel that several additional points need to be made to present a more complete understanding of reconciliation in Africa.

58

EVOLUTION OF PRACTICES IN THE CHRISTIAN TRADITION

It is not necessary to retrace all the historical details of the different forms of penance and reconciliation in the Christian churches. There are many useful texts available.[3] Nonetheless, it would be useful to review some of the highlights, for they will elucidate the questions raised from the African perspective.

The Christian church knew three types of penitential rite. The earliest allowed the remission of such serious sins as homicide, apostasy, adultery, superstitious and demoniac practices, false witness, and so forth. This form of penance was severe. One was removed from the common life of the community and devoted oneself to continual prayer and mortification for one to three years. The return to the community after this period of penance took place during the *Triduum* by a rite of imposition of hands and the removal of the penitential vestment by the bishop. This kind of penance and reconciliation could take place only once in one's life. If a cleric had to undergo this rite, he automatically lost his orders.

The second manner of penance was more direct and less rigid. The priests imposed a mortification—a fine or prayers—on Christians who came to confess their sorrow for having sinned. To facilitate the process, a list of sins was drawn up with a corresponding list of penalties. This manner was repeatable, private, and accessible to all categories of the faithful. It developed in Ireland in the fifth century and quickly spread across the continent, although it never completely replaced the earlier rite. Commutation of penalties degenerated over time into commercial practices. Slowly, one could buy back three years of fasting, for example, by having masses said or by giving a gift of sixty pieces of gold to the church.

The third manner was that of confession. In the thirteenth century the accusation of sin grew in immense proportions as the dominant characteristic of the penitential process. In it the focus on confession as the avowal of sin became the instrument of absolution, overshadowing the humiliating practice of discussing in detail one's sins.

Vatican II brought salutary reforms to a sacrament that had fallen into disuse. It reestablished the communal dimension of the rite and refocused the sacrament on reconciliation. It enlarged the possibilities for the celebration of the sacrament by adding new forms: individual reconciliation; communal reconciliation with confession and individual absolution; and communal reconciliation with communal confession and absolution.[4] One should note the restrictions placed upon the third rite of reconciliation. These include extreme urgency, the impossibility of utilizing the other forms, and the obligation of the penitent whose sins are grave to seek out individual reconciliation later.[5] In case of emergency, only these words must be pronounced by the priest: "And I, in the name of the Father, the Son, and the Holy Spirit, I pardon you of all your sins."

The gesture that accompanies the words of the absolution is one of the early church, the hand placed upon the penitent, who responds, "Amen."

We can deduce several theological principles from this evolution. They will be useful when evaluating the rites developing from African Christian experience. First, one should note that the sacrament of reconciliation of penitents is necessary for the deepening of the baptismal conversion. It is the grace of the Holy Spirit who, in this sacrament, brings to fruition the death and resurrection of Jesus Christ in the Christian, who remains a sinner on this earth. Further, we can state that the forgiveness of God is not limited to this sacrament. Yet through this process of confessing one's faults to the minister of absolution, one can realize the fruits of a sacrament—the gift of God expressed and realized within the human condition. And finally, the sacrament reconciles one both to God and the church. For the church, while being holy, is made up of sinners, and it is tarnished by the sin of each of its members. That is why communal celebrations have been encouraged. But the communal celebrations do not have to take place to the detriment of the personal dimension of conversion and "satisfaction," where one assumes responsibility for the wrong one has committed. It seems clear that the public confession of sin must be supported by individual confession and penance to bring it to its fullest completion.

AFRICA AND THE NEW RITUALS OF PENANCE

Early penitential rites in the West by and large carried on the traditional symbolism of the Jewish world. Shaven heads, the wearing of fringes, and the imposition of ashes are examples. Black Africa, because of the importance of reconciliation to its social groups, offers a panoply of gestures and symbols for consideration as parts of the rite. As B. Adoukonou states in his article on traditional medicine and Christian ministry:

> Because public confession is so important in Africa to the healthy reintegration into community, would we not gain a great deal by not imitating the Occident's practice of the sacrament? This is true especially because the white world has grown more and more indifferent to it. Would it not be better, then, to incorporate African symbolism into the rite and thereby aid the restoration of the Church as a family?[6]

Although we would agree with Adoukonou to some extent, it is important to remain cautious. The whole system within African society needs to be welcomed and evangelized, for it is the forgiveness of God in the church that forms the theological heart of the rite of penance.

Morality for the black African and Bantu in particular is anthropo-
centric.[7] The human person is the aim and point of departure in regard to
salvation and fulfilling the goals of life. All precepts and social organization work to protect and nurture the life of the human person. The person
is viewed as fundamentally good. If someone does something wrong, it is
because of circumstances, because he or she has been "led into error" or
has been imprudent or inattentive to the needs of others. The evil is not
within the person, in this African view, but without, "in the world."
According to traditional African teachings, God did not introduce evil,
although there are some voices that deplore the "incompleteness" of the
work of creation.[8]

If evil comes from outside, then one can track it down, surround it,
fight it, and conquer it. It is not an accident that black Africans are by
nature optimists in the face of the world and its cataclysms. Evil is not
the final explanation of the world for them. It can be excluded from the
heart of the one who has been invaded by it. The penitential formula of
the Congolese (Zairian) mass expresses this conviction: "Lord our God,
just as the leech adheres to the skin and sucks the blood of a person, evil
has invaded us, our life is diminished."[9]

In traditional African teaching, moral fault and sin are fundamentally
faults against one's neighbor, against human beings. As Benezet Bujo
observes:

> The general mentality of black Africa sees evil as coming from man,
> not from God, so that evil lives horizontally, that is to say man to
> man. Many African tribes do not believe that one can offend God.[10]

God is beyond our reach, they would argue; how then could a created
being affect God? Our sin touches those near us, those who are vulner-
able and capable of being hurt. To do evil is to harm our equal. Others
may be wrong in different ways, either directly or through the channel of
their own or their betters. All the same, because of the interdependence of
beings, a fault committed by one member of the family has repercussions
on all members to the point that reparation involves the whole family.

Finally, traditional teaching about sin also includes the belief that sin
twists the normal and habitual order of the universe. This disorder makes
things hobble. In the Luba language any physical handicap is called by
the same word as "fault."

Repairing wrongs done is first of all a community affair. A wrong,
once committed, even in private, is a disorder that is introduced into the
universe and the social tissue. Therefore, its repair must be public. This is
not to say that every repair of a wrong involves the whole village and all
the people. It would usually be sufficient to have some representatives
from the groups of those concerned.

The process of repair in African societies begins with the unmasking. Discussions about culpability and responsibilities of those involved are finished before the rite occurs. In addition, a determination has been made as to what action is needed to return to the right order and to reestablish the equilibrium that has been ruptured by the wrong. At the rite of reconciliation, the one at fault steps forward and makes a confession, in the presence of the injured parties or their representatives. Depending on the wrong that had been committed, he or she will, for example, speak a good word to replace the bad that had been said. It could be the paying of a fine or a gesture of self-abasement and humiliation for having scoffed at an elder.

An example of how this works may be helpful. I take one from the year 1986, when a principal medical assistant died in Kinshasa. His eldest son was a doctor whose wife had never gotten along with her father-in-law. It was known, in fact, that she had made malevolent statements against him. After leaving the morgue, the funeral procession was directed toward the home of the eldest son. It stopped a dozen meters away from the entrance so that the repair of the wrong could take place. On her knees the daughter-in-law crawled to the coffin, asked forgiveness of the dead man, and paid a sum of money to the man's brothers. Only then could the coffin be carried onto the son's property.

The final stage in the process is the return to communion, often symbolized by a communal meal as a feast of reunion or by a gesture of communion. In central Africa there is a variety of gestures.[11] For example, both belligerents may drink from the same cup, or one drinks water from the other's jar or eats something that comes from the other. Perhaps they might wash their hands in the same basin. In this case an herb will have been placed in the water and, as they wash, the water swirls and an elder speaks. The water is then spilled on the ground or on the roof. If the belligerents had vowed never to see each other again until death, they might descend into a hole dug for the occasion. Together they would lie down in the hole, simulating death and burial, and then rise up together speaking positively.

If there had been a conflict between two tribes where there had been killings, the rite might involve the immolation of a human or an animal life. The two peoples would meet at a common meeting place. The animal chosen was often a dog; it would be killed with blows from their fists and feet. The animal would then be dismembered by hand. Knives were not permitted. The meat would be grilled and eaten after everyone present had been given a piece. There are isolated cases in Luba history of human sacrifice to accomplish the reconciliation of peoples, in which cases the person to be sacrificed was buried alive after his legs and arms had been broken.[12]

TOWARD AN AFRICAN CHRISTIAN RITE OF RECONCILIATION

We have seen that the Black African view of sin was essentially social and horizontal. In our catechesis in Africa we must first underline the fact that wrong committed against one's neighbor is evil because it does not accord with the plan of God for the neighbor and that it is possible for the human person to interfere with God's plan. This does not necessarily invalidate the Black African concept of the world or its anthropology. Rather, it enlarges its perspective and opens new horizons.

Second, the African catalog of sins must be integrated into Christian life with the appropriate alterations. The primacy of the love of God and the love of neighbor is a central principle in that process. Such African expressions as "I have sinned but I did no wrong" witnesses to the urgency of this integration.

Throughout history, the sacrament of penance has been presented as a preparation for the eucharist.[13] No doubt confession prior to the reception of the eucharist can be justified. However, when we raise questions about presenting the sacrament of penance to the African church, we must allow this sacrament to stand on its own. It must be seen not merely in relation to the eucharist but principally in relation to one's entire life of faith.

Optimism about human nature is a part of African tradition; the excesses of this attitude need attention to make clear the reality of human weakness and the continual need for conversion. From my perspective, the Christian tradition brings a new image of the human—as a being who is capable of doing both good and evil, a being who must mortify himself or herself and do penance in order to adhere to God's plan and regain God's image and likeness. In summary, one could say that we are always in need of salvation. This invites our African peoples to reorganize their universe. If humans are important in this vast universe, it is because we are made in the image and likeness of God. Our "anthropocentrism" should lead us to discover the code of God in humanity. This discovery means that the laws and interdicts of our ancestors must be harmonized with the plan of salvation in Christ. In my opinion, this process can ideally be deepened when, on the one hand, Christianity welcomes the African rites of reconciliation, and, on the other, when these rites are reoriented to Christ and his message.

RITES OF RECONCILIATION IN AFRICA

It would be useful now to turn to some examples of the way the rite of reconciliation has been inculturated in Africa. The first example I wish to give is from my own experience in a base community. In a region where there are several traditional chiefs who vie for power and control, I had asked the local civil administration for a piece of "autonomous" land outside of the control of any traditional chiefs' groups. This was to safeguard the community against being caught in the middle of their rivalries. The parish church, presbytery, schools, maternity clinic, dispensary, and some housing for teachers and other faithful were all located in this autonomous space. Since it did not fall under the authority of any chief, conflict resolution required a different mode of operation. The founding principle was, We will resolve all our conflicts in a Christian manner.

This served the goal of setting an example for all the people of the way in which Christian faith liberates people and can be a force for an abundant life in love. It was within this framework that rituals of reconciliation emerged.

When a conflict arose between two individuals, the responsible members of the community brought the two parties together in the presence of two other community elders. Together they determined the respective responsibility of each party to the conflict. They identified the causes and prescribed penalties. Later they would convene those involved for a day of reconciliation. That day would begin with a reading from the word of God. After having commented on the reading, the responsible community leader gave each belligerent a moment to speak. Each recognized his error publicly. Then, spitting on the ground, each renounced vengeance and hatred. The guilty one would have brought along the assigned fine and tea and milk. He would then share them with all assembled, after having sipped tea from the same cup as his antagonist. If the damage had been great, the community would make the guilty party promise to restore what had been lost. If there had been an injury or illness, the expense of the medical care would be the responsibility of the one responsible. And, as a sign of his good will, a third or a half of the payment would be made at that time. A song of thanksgiving would be sung and a final prayer said by the responsible party. Then they would disperse.

This is not a sacramental reconciliation, but the Christians hold it in high esteem, especially when a priest is present for the ritual. We have tried to correct the excessiveness of the communal dimension of the ritual by adding the readings of God's word, thus underlining the notion that forgiveness is a grace received from God.

Another example is a rite performed in a restrained and intimate group. Under the guidance of the priest, readings and songs begin the rite. After the gospel the priest offers reflections on the gospel, followed by a moment of silence. Then the priest asks each one to confess. They stand in a circle around the altar. Each one in turn moves and kneels before the altar and speaks aloud his sins and failings. After the confession is over, a basin filled with water is placed before the altar. The celebrant blesses the water using the prayers of blessing of the Roman rite, imploring the power of the Holy Spirit to purify all who dip their hands in the water as a sign of repentance. In turn, the penitents come and dip their hands into the basin saying:

> Lord, through your mercy, make my sins drown in this water, so my life becomes once again, as it was at the time of my baptism, a song of praise to you, and a grace to my brothers and sisters.

When they have finished, the priest pronounces a formula of general absolution. They sing a song of thanksgiving, while the priest takes the basin of dirty water and throws it outside, saying, "As this water disappears, may it take away all sins that poison our life and our community." The priest then asks for silent prayer. The Our Father and the kiss of peace follow. A song closes the celebration.

The reconciliation of a sorcerer is a rite that responds to an important dimension of life in Africa.[14] In the past the church has tried simply to dismiss sorcery as vain beliefs and superstitions. In reality, however, this is like covering burning cinders with ashes. Today, pastoral practice is different, and sorcery is seen as an incarnation of evil, in which its spells are pernicious and sometimes fatal. However, the power of Christ is presented as able to stand against it.

The sorcerer is part of a coven that knows how to provoke and channel the interaction of spiritual forces. Instead of using these forces for good, the sorcerer turns them into a catastrophe for his neighbor. This evil is not innate in the person, for, as it is said, "People are not born sorcerers; they *become* sorcerers." This happens through the evil of other sorcerers who prey upon the weaknesses of fragile men and women to deceive them. Such a man is dangerous to the community, and his reconciliation involves "vomiting" out the sorcery in a rite of purification. The gospel and Christian prayer are presented as forces for liberation, and Christians turn to them to expel the evil that contaminates the sorcerer.

Charismatic prayer is by far the most successful against sorcery. The experiences of Monsignor Milingo in Zambia, of Father Lufuluabo in Kasai, of Abbé Kibwila in Kinshasa, of Abbé Kasongo in Shaba, of Father Hebga and Eric de Rosny in Cameroon give evidence to the role of charismatic prayer. Their rituals include the imposition of hands accompanied by prayer, sometimes including the sprinkling of holy water.

The parish priest of Karabe, in East Africa, proceeds differently. He assembles the faithful of the village and other sympathizers. Then he retires with the one involved in sorcery for an individual confession that is *not* followed by absolution. The penitent sorcerer rejoins the assembly to confess his guilt and seek forgiveness for the wrongs he has committed against the community. As a sign of regret and of his decision to no longer be taken in by evil, he lets fall to the ground all the instruments of his diabolic operations—those things that served to give him power over victims, including a small pot used to mix his macabre dishes.

The celebrant interrogates the assembly: "Do you want N. reconciled to the community?"

The assembly responds, "Yes, provided that he renounces all of his witchcraft and that he pays a fine."

The penitent then swears to desist from these acts of sorcery. The oath may take different forms according to the location and the one involved—for example, simple words with anathema or straddling a cross. The assembly applauds and greets the oath. Then the penitent places his fine, usually a goat and a beverage, at the foot of the altar. This is followed by the celebration of the eucharist and a community meal put on by the penitent according to his means. Sometimes part of the fine is reckoned as the expense of the meal.

For further examples of rituals of reconciliation in Africa, it is useful to turn to the independent churches. We find in the independent churches that the oath taken is public, but it is not always explicit or personal. It is often followed by abstinence in the form of refraining from taking food and alcoholic beverages. Vigils of prayer for different lengths of time can follow. In Zimbabwe, the Reverend Willy Mnyagatwa followed a traditional rite of reconciliation, which he felt was the only one that truly touched the lives of the faithful.

The way of reconciling spouses is particularly interesting. It takes place inside the couple's home. One of the elders of the husband is present, as well as the Christian community. At sunset they kill a chicken or a goat (depending on the means of the couple), and the blood of the animal is sprinkled on the doorstep of their house. The pastor, after having prayed for the grace of forgiveness from God, has the two belligerents pass through the door. Inside the house the family elder gives advice and ends with an invitation for the couple to join hands. The pastor prays for the strengthening of this reconciliation. The community outdoors proclaims its support with songs and acclamations.[15]

Distinctive in all of these rites is the effort to synthesize the ancient and the modern. We have taken a brief look at traditional African rites of reconciliation, as well as at the evolution of the rites of the Christian tradition in Africa. In all these examples we see three parts: the community, the avowal, and the repair or the bond. If we look first at the community's involvement in the process, we see how central this is to the traditional African conception of world. Every being is linked to the life of all others, and a diminution of any life endangers all others. This has been true since the beginning of human life on earth. A wrong that introduces disharmony has the power to provoke a chain reaction. The fault of one concerns the whole. Thus the community must be present when there is a moment of reconciliation.

The manner in which the community is present varies according to the situation. The whole community can be gathered if the situation is serious. This is the case in something like sorcery. Often, though, it is enough to have several representatives. The elders of the families have traditionally held an important place in rites of reconciliation. They represent the roots of the community, the ancestors. They have to be invited and can contribute significantly. But the Christian community, with its ministers, has to play a primary leadership role because it adds the unique revelation of God's forgiveness and grace. The prominence of the Christian community is not intended to usurp the place of the elders. It is meant, rather, to enlarge the perspective. The clan lives on the ladder of the church. The penitent has not created disharmony only in a single family but to those united by the blood of Christ in the church. So, the participants at this reconciliation are not only those related by blood but also those who share in the new life in Christ. The "elder" of the Christian community presides, drawing the elders by blood into association with the community.

The word in fact corresponds to a fundamental element of oral civilizations. The word is not only a means or a tool, it is like a person, it is alive. Oaths and avowals participate in the dynamism of the word. Expressing one's fault reverses what was bad and disastrous. Our growing traditions, nevertheless, do not insist that the avowal always take place before the entire community. It suffices that legitimate representatives of the community be present and that the avowal be declared in clear detail.

A community celebration does not lead necessarily to a collective absolution. There is no need to infringe upon the canons concerning communal absolution. A simple gesture by the priest suffices as he imposes hands on each penitent as he or she kneels before the altar making the oath. In communities where a priest does not reside, a rite of renunciation of evil could take place without the imposition of hands. A minister (not a priest) then presides over the readings and the avowal. He then pours a bit of holy water in a basin full of water, and then the penitents will come forward to wash their hands. The basin will be emptied outdoors as prayers for the grace of purification are said.

The power of these prayers for forgiveness is clear. God does not limit forgiveness to sacraments alone. The effectiveness of a rite of reconciliation outside of the sacrament of penance does not in any way diminish the privileged place of the sacraments in the economy of salvation.

In all traditional rites of reconciliation the payment of a fine is imposed on the culpable party or on both belligerents. There are times when the chastisement is too severe. Take, for instance, the case of a thief who repeats his crimes and has his hands burned; or when a female adulteress is paraded nude through the village; or when a sorcerer is killed or exiled from the community. These excesses, however cruel, should not discredit the whole system. A punishment or a fine makes the offender fully responsible for his or her actions.

The forgiveness of God is one of the summits of Christian revelation. It is a pardon through love that is continually offered and always waiting for the sinner. God is not an avenger who will make us pay for our sins. Nonetheless, for this pardon to be beneficial for us, we must welcome it. That is the way we must think of repentance. And our repentance never exacts God's forgiveness, for God's forgiveness always remains gratuitous.

The notion of pardon is hardly present in our traditional rites, and so this is the way in which Christian belief and practice effect change in the ritual life of the community. Readings from the Bible, prayers explicitly asking for the grace of God's forgiveness and for the forgiveness of the people, one for the other, must be emphasized. Taking care that fines do not become heavy burdens should also be a part of Christian reconciliation. And finally, the celebration of the eucharist binds Christian and traditional practices of reconciliation in a unique way. Not only does the communal meal function as a powerful symbol across cultural differences, but in the case of reconciliation the Christian meaning shines through. It is the sacrifice of Christ that becomes the guarantee of reconciliation.

5

Marrying in Christ

It is not within the limits of this chapter to review in a systematic and comprehensive fashion the entire evolutionary development of the rites of matrimony. There are excellent resources that do chart the course of change in the sacrament of matrimony through ancient and medieval history to our own day.[1] Nonetheless, in a short overview we will discuss some relevant aspects of the history of the Christian marriage to better situate the African context.

"Christians marry just like everyone else." This attestation comes from the famous letter to Diogenes,[2] and constitutes the first evidence that the church had not invented the rite of the celebration of marriage. The church took the local elements of the celebration from the customs of the people and sometimes assumed the ancient practices and sometimes eliminated or altered elements or symbols.

Greco-Roman marriage was characterized by the following elements: a veil that the groom placed on the bride; a crown of myrtle or of orange; consulting the gods to know whether they were favorable; reading the contract in the presence of witnesses; mutually exchanging consent between the partners; joining hands, which signified the passage of the bride from her father's care to her husband's; the sacrifice to the gods; the marriage feast; the procession, which accompanied the bride to the bridal chamber.

Christians made certain changes in this ritual. Among these changes, they abandoned practices that were contrary to their faith, such as the rites of divination, the sacrifice to the gods, and some licentious gestures that took place during the procession to the bridal chamber.[3] They invited the ministers of the church to participate in these celebrations. The presence of these ministers brought the practice of prayers of blessing, in particular, requests for the fruitfulness and growth of the couple. There were liturgical songs, psalms, and readings from the Sacred Scriptures. Over a long period of time the church introduced its own legislation on

marriage and elaborated the theological principles on which that legislation was based. One example of this legislation was the prohibition of
divorce on the theological principle that the marriage of Christians is a
sign of the union of Christ and the church[4]; the gift of the grace of God as
the bond that holds together this human union[5]; and the invitation to
imitate the model of love given in the Sacred Scriptures. Finally, the church
articulated the teaching that Christian marriage prefigured heavenly marriages.[6]

Diversity of rites and practices existed among the churches in spite of
efforts that began in the fourth and fifth centuries to standardize them.
We see in Milan and Rome, for example, that the aspect that dominated
the marriage rite was the veil, the *velatio-nuptiali*s.[7] Gaul, Spain, and the
Celtic countries were noted for their rites of blessing of the couple in the
bridal chamber—the *benedictio in thalamo*—with the exchange of a kiss
and the ring.[8] Christians in the East adopted the rite of crowning, and the
Byzantine rite of marriage was commonly called the "office of corona-
tion,"[9] in an emphasis that has carried down right until the present.

The ritual location of the celebration of matrimony also has varied
throughout the ages. Certain churches celebrated it before or during the
eucharist with prayers and invocations for the marital bond. Similarly,
the words of the priest and the spouses varied from church to church,
sometimes emphasizing the consent of the spouses,[10] sometimes the blessing of the priest and God—which became the rule after the Council of
Trent.[11] This council, in spite of its polemic against the Reformers for
denying the sacramentality of Christian marriage, also wished to guard
the diversity of the customs and ceremonies accompanying marriage.[12]

Vatican II maintained this concern,[13] while presenting a model that
would be used by different episcopal conferences.[14] This Vatican II model
establishes a format that can be celebrated within the eucharist or as a
separate celebration, although it must always be preceded by scriptural
readings and a homily.[15] The format involves:

- questioning the fiancees, who hold hands (this demonstrating a
  different emphasis—the communion of the couple and not the
  passage of bride from father to husband).
- the exchange of consent by the spouses and the reception of the
  consent by the minister.
- blessing and exchange of the wedding rings, which reminds them
  to love each other faithfully.
- blessing the couple—which is done between the Our Father and
  the sign of peace.

The readings and prayers of the new rite express different aspects of
the mystery of Christian marriage as understood in the tradition, for
example, that marriage conforms to the divine plan, that the unity of the
couple is a sign that their marriage represents the Kingdom and the way
of life that the gospel portrays for the couple. The legislation of the church

has always emphasized that procreation and the good of the spouses are the ends of marriage. Vatican II defined marriage as a "partnership of the whole of life and love," while recalling that children are its "crown."[16]

TRADITIONAL AFRICAN MARRIAGE

Vatican II stipulated that the priest and/or deacon who is assisting at the marriage must ask for and receive the consent of the partners; this is the fundamental disposition asked by Vatican II for all Christian marriage ceremonies.[17] This will be the point of comparison between traditional African marriage customs and marriage customs that developed in the East and West under the responsibility of the Christian churches. Marriage in Black Africa is first of all a bond that, through the union of two persons, a man and a woman, seals an alliance between the two families to which the partners belong.[18] This communal character of marriage responds to the communal way of life in all Black Africa. Second, because this union is where life blossoms and grows, the whole of society attends to it in a special way. At the marriage ceremony this is shown in rites of harmonization and rites for the prevention of evil. Third, traditional African teaching about marriage is in harmony with Christian teaching, which emphasized the centrality of procreation.

A distinguishing characteristic of traditional African teaching on marriage is the perception that marrying is a *dynamic process*, not something that happens in a single moment. It begins with the promises of marriage at engagement and ends with the birth of the first child. The gift of a dowry is a powerful symbol of marriage in African society. The dowry is called "the symbol of alliance" given by the family that receives the female to the family that allows one of its members to leave. In fact, the receiving family never stops "giving" the dowry, because it never finishes giving thanks for such a great gift.

In traditional African teaching, marriage is not indissoluble. It is understood that shipwrecks are possible in the course of human life: bad treatment by one of the partners, the unkindness or malevolence of one family, the discovery of sorcery, sterility, misconduct, death, and all that is opposed to life can all be causes of dissolution.

AFRICAN CHRISTIAN MARRIAGE

In Africa today, Christians who marry continue to sit astride two worlds: the traditional and the occidental Christian. This coexistence is not always peaceful. The fundamentally communal nature of marriage according to African culture sometimes conflicts with the contractual and individual perspective of the other. Also, the centrality of fertility in the African understanding of marriage does not hold the same power in the Christian definition of marriage. And, the African perception of marriage as a dynamic process does not match Scholastic theology's teaching that the sacrament of marriage occurs at one certain moment. These three points alone have generated a great deal of controversy on the pastoral level in Black African Christianity. Certain leaders have maintained the position of occidental Scholastic theology in making the "economy of salvation" coincide with the sacramental organization of the Roman Catholic Church.[19] There are others who recognize the validity of the two systems and therefore acknowledge that there are variations in the nature of marriage itself. They would admit that there are Christian marriages that are not necessarily sacraments, for example, marriages that are moving through the traditional process of marrying, certain polygamous marriages, remarriages after divorce.[20]

Concretely, the church must recognize the validity of traditional marriage for Christians, admitting these married Christians to the sacraments and not insisting that all Christians under penalty of sin must have a sacramental marriage. Indissoluble and unique, Christian marriage must be seen as a vocation in the church, a mission. Otherwise, in the case of sterility for example, to not permit remarriage threatens the very foundation of a culture that places primary importance on fertility because it is essential for survival.[21]

There is evidence of slow change in these customs in Africa as well as in the West. I doubt that questions will be resolved with Africans being totally converted to the notion of "marriage-for-love," an individual contract, or an eschatological view of marriage, as some have suggested.[22] Christian churches in the fifth and sixth centuries did not universally define marriage as a sacrament. Yet they had a vision of marriage that was celebrated and lived in a Christian manner. It was experienced as an institution in which one could encounter the grace of God. Similarly, I believe that certain dimensions of the celebrations in African communities contribute to clarifying the theological understanding of life and to building up faith. In the same way that one does not *understand* walking theoretically but learns it through the experience of walking, or learns language through talking, perhaps it is not necessary to have everything theoretically resolved before commencing on a path of dialogue and adaptation of the theology and practice of Christian marriage in Africa.

EXAMPLES OF AFRICAN CELEBRATION OF MARRIAGE

African Christian marriages begin with traditional customs. They end with a Christian marriage in the complete sense as fulfillment of these cultural understandings. One sees numerous parallels between the two understandings as well as many points of difference. In the beginning, "a man shall leave his father and mother and be joined to his wife" (Mt 19:5). Does this mean that the husband and wife walk away from and ignore their responsibilities to their respective families once they are married? It seems to me that the African communal spirit is an advantage for an ecclesiology of communion.[23] This corresponds with the Black African understanding of the world as a place of participation in the total mystery of life. The traditional Christian prayer of blessing over the bride accords perfectly with the African concern for fertility. The fact that marriage is progressively concluded in Africa, instead of being a problem, could help the world church think critically about notions of sacraments as an instantaneous change. Thus Africa may have a contribution to make to the West in its current difficulties over marriage and divorce. From the African usages, one sees a consciousness that finds sacramentality in all the great stages of life.

We can review some of the significant developments in the celebration of marriage in Africa. In 1977 Aylward Shorter presented a number of tentative proposals in the *African Ecclesiastical Review*. In 1979 Monsignor Mukeng'a Kalond, bishop of Luiza, proposed the *Rituel Luba* (2d edition) as an outline for celebrating marriage; it followed the Roman ritual of Vatican II while adopting terminology and gestures common in Black Africa. For example, the two families are called on to speak during the exchange of consent. The spouses place their hand on the bible when they pronounce their vows. The ritual suggests that white kaolin be used for the anointing by the parents and the minister of the church, and it suggests that practical advice be given to the spouses at the end of the rite.[24]

The questions that open the exchange of consent are original and read as follows:

Priest: *(To the woman)* Who have you brought to us?

Woman: He is my husband.

Priest: Do you love him?

Woman: Yes, I love him.

Priest: *(To the man)* Who have you brought to us?

Man: She is my wife.

Priest: Do you love her?

Man: Yes, I love her.[25]

Then the following questions are posed to the parents.

Priest: What do you have to say about the sacrament your children will receive?

Parents: We who have brought into the world N. share this sacrament in communion with N. Our only desire is that God bless them, so that they will live in joy and communion, that they will be fertile and give our names to their children, and that they will nurture their children to grow, just as we nurtured them. We pray that God will protect them.

The vows spoken by each spouse (after the series of interrogations in the Roman Missal) follow:

Before God and before this assembly, I (N.) promise firmly to hold my "wife of this sacrament" until the day I die. I renounce with all my heart the act of taking other wives. I place my hand on the Holy Book so that if I break my promise, God may punish me according to his will.[26]

In 1983 a group of Christian lay people offered several ritual elements for insertion in the liturgical celebrations of marriage.[27] They envision the Christian ritual following all the stages of Bantu marriage (i.e., the offering of the first part of the dowry; the first visit of the woman to the family of the man; the installation of the new couple in their dwelling; and the birth of the first child). At each stage the action is to be accompanied by the word of God, the prayer of the community, and the blessing of the church. When the dowry is presented, the sprinkling of white kaolin over the gifts expresses the request that "these gifts be a channel of communion between the two families." When the woman is welcomed into the family of the man, the priest or the "elder" should be among those who attend. He says a prayer asking "that the Lord who probes the loins and the heart help this woman and the family who welcomes her to understand each other, to come to know each other, and to value one another as the church has taught in the gospel. That their eyes may be open and that they will see how they are called to live together."

When the couple are installed in their dwelling, a blessing of the spouses and a solemn exchange of consent should take place in the parish church. This affords the extended family opportunity to participate. Symbols of their union and of love should be shown. The following are examples: having the couple sit together on a mat in front of the altar; exchanging a pestle given by the husband to the wife and a small mortar given by the wife to the husband. Finally, at the birth of the first child, there should be a ceremony for the solemn vow of faithful, sacramental love understood as the fullness of the marriage as sign of the love of God for God's people and as a sign of the fidelity of Christ to his church. Several lay people suggested that this stage should be accompanied by a solemn pact of blood between the two spouses. In that pact each spouse's finger would be pricked and they would let their blood slowly drip into a chalice that contains wine for the eucharist that they will drink at communion. This ceremony would be reserved for those who are judged to have received a special calling to live a marriage that serves as a special example of the steadfast love of Christ for the church.

In North Cameroon, at the final stage of the process the two partners cut a piece of cord, which serves as a sign of "no return" in the marriage. This is based on the fact that when one cuts a cord it can never return to its original form. In the culture of the Cameroon going against such a vow would be to risk death.[28]

In Burundi, between 1969 and 1974, Lucien Birahinduka experimented with a liturgical arrangement that emphasized the communal character of African marriage. The parents on both sides played a role in the ceremony. Their gestures translated the customary blessings of their community to the couple. In Tanzania, between 1969 and 1982, several parishes worked within the same framework and tried to provide a way for the families to transmit their local customs within the Christian celebration. The chief representatives of the two families stood before the altar with the two partners. They spoke to confirm their support of the union, and the priest sprinkled white kaolin on the partners.

I will take my last example of liturgical developments in African Christian marriage ceremonies from the Congo. A. Duteil records the following description:

> The traditional marriage ceremony takes place on the mat, that is to say, the fiancé and fiancée take their places, seated next to one another. The money and the keg of beer, which are part of the dowry, are at his side. Then a series of rites take place that we have taken up in the Christian celebration so that the sacrament can be lived and signified more profoundly. Once the fiancees are seated on the mat in front of the altar, the father of the groom and the mother of the bride give their blessing by means of a traditional plant placed in their hands. This blessing by the parents is extremely important in Africa and it situates the marriage in the great movement of life itself, which has come down through the ancestors.
>
> In the village, one gives a glass of wine to the bride. If she gives it to his father, then she has accepted the son as her husband. And the father asks her the traditional question, "This wine, will it make me vomit?" The bride reassures him, and then the father drinks it. For the Christian celebration, the young woman offers the chalice to the priest. The priest accepts in the name of God. Then, according to the tradition, the fiancees exchange a sip of wine. To celebrate this ceremony in the midst of a eucharist would greatly increase its meaning, because it is no longer wine that is shared by the spouses but the blood of Christ. Christians understand very well that they are marrying in the death and resurrection of Christ so as to live in his love. There is no need for lengthy explanations. The rite speaks for itself. It comes from the heart of the culture of the Congo.[29]

6

Celebrating the Solace
of the Sick

The sacrament of the sick has evolved not only because of awareness that the church ought to be involved in the suffering of those who are sick and in the death of the Christian, but also because medical science has been involved in illness. Realizing that before the twentieth century serious illness was almost always terminal, it is understandable that the rites surrounding serious illness were obsessed with death, to the point that the rite received the designation "extreme unction" or the "last rites."

THE EVOLUTION OF THE SACRAMENT OF THE SICK
IN THE WEST

The history of the Christian church's rites for the sick is rooted in the writings of the New Testament, where Christ showed his concern and solicitude for the sick. "And there was a leper who came to him, and knelt before him, saying, 'Lord, if you choose, you can make me clean.' He stretched out his hand and touched him, saying, 'I do choose. Be made clean!'" (Mt 8:2-3). The apostles anointed the sick with oil and cured them (Mk 6:13).

St. James gives evidence of a later practice dating from apostolic times: "Are any among you sick? They should call for the elders of the church and have them pray over them, anointing them with oil in the name of the Lord. The prayer of faith will save the sick, and the Lord will raise them up; and anyone who has committed sins will be forgiven" (Jas 5:14-15).

From the third century to the seventh century prayers for the blessing of oil and water for the rite of anointing the sick give evidence of the continuation of the practice. But these prayers also show confusion between anointing catechumens and anointing the sick. Here are some extracts:

> Just as in sanctifying this oil, O God, you give holiness to those who are anointed with it and who receive it, this oil with which you have anointed the kings, the priests, and the prophets assures the comfort of those who experience it and the health of those who use it (Hippolytus of Rome, *The Apostolic Tradition*).

> You who cure every illness and suffering, who have given the gift of healing to those you judged worthy of it: send over this oil, which is the type of your sweetness, the fullness of your mercy so that it may free those who suffer. Restore the sick to health. Sanctify those who are converted and come to your faith, because you are strong and praiseworthy forever (*Testament of the Lord*).

In such prayers we discern the text of James beneath the surface pointing to two effects of the anointing: physical healing and forgiveness of sins. Still, they do not tell us anything about the development of the rite. The canons of Hippolytus, in clarifying the meaning of the text from the *Apostolic Tradition,* recall two gestures—imposing hands and anointing—made by the priest or bishop. But in other places Christians are known to have received this anointing and to have applied it to themselves when they were ill. They are also reported to have performed the anointing while drinking consecrated or holy water.[1]

In the Eastern church the same elements are mentioned; but with a particular insistence on the presence of several priests concelebrating, and the mention—in addition to the imposition of hands and the anointing—of imposing the Book of the Gospels on the sick person. The oil used was oil from the lamp that had been lit for the celebration.

In the monasteries of the West these rites became surprisingly elaborate. First, the ritual of visiting the sick includes numerous psalms and antiphons, sprinkling with holy water, confession of the sick person, prayers for reconciliation before death, imposing hands, readings, a profession of faith, and reception of communion by the sick person. The anointings varied in number in the various rituals, but they were all grouped around the five senses.

From the fifteenth century onward, the rituals began to be called *extreme unction* because most celebrations of the ritual for the sick were connected with the reconciliation (confession) and rituals for the dying one. Since then, the emphasis of the prayers, which had originally been directed to the healing of the sick person, was more and more directed toward preparation for death. Healing was almost exclusively interpreted as a spiritual healing of sin and interior purification. Thus a sacrament destined for the gravely ill came to be reserved for those about to die. It should be mentioned as well that this ecclesiastical evolution was taking place parallel to evolution in the practice of medicine. As that began to change, alterations in the church's views might have been expected.

The ritual edited in 1614 assumed much of an earlier Franciscan ritual that had attempted to shorten the rite. It included sprinkling, confession, psalms and readings, prayers, anointings, and, finally, reception of communion. Later, however, communion *preceded* the anointing, which was considered the last act in the drama of death. A distinction was made between visiting the sick and anointing the sick. Practically speaking, this 1614 ritual was adopted in the new edition of the ritual in 1925, and it was used until Vatican II.

THE PRESENT RITUAL OF ANOINTING THE SICK

Vatican II preferred the title "anointing the sick" to that of the Council of Trent, "extreme unction." In addition, its formulation of the prayers underscored the teaching that the sacrament involves a grace of the Holy Spirit and that the effects are the forgiveness of sins and spiritual healing, as well as the relief and physical cure of the sick person. Concerning the number of anointings, it was recommended that they normally not exceed two, although the possibility was left that—according to the circumstances and the symbolism of healing in each culture—more could be administered.[2] The oil of the anointing of the sick could be any vegetable oil. The imposition of hands was to take place in silence. Thus the principal gestures of the sacrament would be the imposition of hands and anointing.

The following is the outline of the ritual when celebrated outside of mass: (1) a greeting of peace and an instruction from the priest; (2) sprinkling with holy water, during which all make the sign of the cross, and a prayer; (3) a penitential rite, during which the sick person may make his or her confession; (4) reading from scripture; (5) recitation of a litany for the sick; (6) the imposition of hands; (7) anointing with holy oil: (a) a prayer of thanksgiving (or of blessing), and (b) anointing of the forehead and the hands; (8) general intercessions and prayer; (9) recitation of the Our Father (which may be followed by holy communion); (10) a final blessing by the priest.

If the sacrament is celebrated during the eucharist, the ritual begins with the litany for the sick and ends with the general intercessions and the prayer. The ritual provides several choices of texts and various prayer formulas for different kinds of illness and situations.

The liturgy of the sick also includes rituals of preparation for death, of viaticum, and for funerals. However, we will not consider them here, given the fact that they go beyond the scope of the present work.

CULTURAL ISSUES SURROUNDING THE ANOINTING
OF THE SICK IN BLACK AFRICA

Before asking questions about ways of celebrating, let us define what sickness means in African cultures. In Bantu Africa sickness represents a lack of harmony and balance, a disorder introduced into the social and cosmic fabric. This disorder is viewed as resulting from different causes. It can arise out of human imprudence following, for example, frequenting a contaminated place, or from dirtiness, neglect, and so forth. It can result as well from bad will from an enemy who might have introduced a bad germ in us. It can result, finally, from beyond—from God or the ancestors—as a warning or as a punishment.

If illness is discovered to have resulted from ordinary and visible causes, one has recourse to ordinary remedies in the visible order, using medicines and the like. A different level of concern occurs when an illness is not "ordinary." In such cases, the persistence of sickness serves as an alarm and demands an in-depth search for another level of causes. The total life of the individual and the group is examined. Often causes like a lack of love or anger on the part of a relative who feels he or she has been offended are found somewhere.

Treatment of sickness, in similar fashion, can occur on two levels. The visible causes call for an ordinary healing by means of plants and other natural elements. An illness by supernatural causes enjoins another level of cure—for example, reconciling members of the family, group or village, but also making a special appeal to forces beyond the visible. Such an appeal in traditional African society is accompanied by invoking the protection of "a strong one"—a divine healer, who may be either male or female.

With this in mind, how should the church understand and symbolize her taking responsibility for the sick? How can she symbolize the message of this sacrament meant for the comforting of the sick and the remission of sins?

First of all, taking into account the African mindset, we should not wait until sickness becomes serious before having recourse to the church, because a slight fever could be an early warning of impending disaster. The church should say to her members, "Come to the sacrament of the sick each time you feel a threat to life." Moreover, taking responsibility for illness by our churches should not be limited to this particular form of celebration. A prayer of comfort for the sick should be organized regularly,[3] including the imposition of hands and, above all, holy water should be given to the sick to drink or it should be sprinkled on them. This symbolism dovetails perfectly with traditional symbols of healing and spiritual therapy where healers use sprinklings and drink.

An African Christian ritual might be structured as follows: (1) readings from scripture; (2) exhortations and requests for pardon from God; (3) prayers of praise; (4) hymns and canticles to the Holy Spirit; (5) blessing of water; (6) the imposition of hands by the priest; (7) a request for and taking a little holy water; (8) a song of thanksgiving; (9) general intercessions; and (10) recitation of the Our Father and a concluding prayer.

Anointing would be reserved for those particular cases when the priest should visit the home. There he would use the rite above.

ABBÉ TSHINYAMA AND THE SICK

I have been present at a rite employed in the Diocese of Kananga by Abbé Boniface Tshinyama. This ritual astutely used a combination of symbols, both local and from elsewhere. It is worth describing in detail, in the place where it took birth, at Kabwe.[4] Kabwe was already famous in colonial times for having two seminaries for the formation of native priests. After the 1960s its importance and renown were diminished when Catholic houses of religious formation were scattered widely. Then, in 1988, there occurred a great rush of sick people toward Kabwe. The cause was that the pastor of the parish, a priest in his forties, Boniface Tshinyama, came to be known as a healer. More recently this rush has subsided, and the events are less spectacular, which affords us the chance to better analyze what was going on.

In Africa, where the mortality rate is among the highest in the world and the average life expectancy is around forty, a special gift of healing takes on vital importance. There are, to be sure, hospitals and dispensaries in Congo (Zaire). They benefit people with the knowledge and techniques of modern medicine, and the Bantus do not disdain them. On the contrary, they flock to them. But they know too well their limitations. In the interests of making a fair comparison, it should not be forgotten that modern medicine has found remedies for only about 25 percent of the illnesses diagnosed to date. For the 75 percent that remain, medicine gropes to retard the illness and to limit damage in the organism so other healing processes can occur. Therapies that have recourse to supernatural means inspire confidence in African people. Research in the West on the effects of meditation, faith, and prayer makes one aware that it is not only Africans who know the benefits of the supernatural.

The personality of Abbé Tshinyama and his spiritual journey are not to be neglected for an understanding of the events of Kabwe. While still in the seminary, he was discovered to have special gifts. During a football match one of his teammates fell, badly injuring his foot. Seeing his teammate lying on the ground with a sprained ankle, Tshinyama touched the painful joint with his hands. His fellow player got better immediately. For those who complained of headaches, he took their head in both his hands and progressively stomped the pain into the ground. The rector of the seminary was made aware of these gifts, and he formally forbade the young man to pursue such therapies.

When Tshinyama was ordained a priest, he was sent to Canada to study. While he was earning his degree in physics and electronics, he met a Canadian religious who was known for his divination practices. During a session, this religious had Abbé Tshinyama stretch his hand over a metal bracelet. As he moved his hand horizontally, the bracelet followed it. His particular gifts were being confirmed, and the Canadian religious encouraged him to use them for the growth of the Kingdom of God.

Since then, visions have joined an interior voice to call him to exercise his gifts for the Kingdom and to make his priesthood fertile. I personally met Boniface in Canada. He enjoyed a very comfortable life there that few blacks even in North America knew. People envisioned that he would find it difficult to return to the poverty and the sorry state of administration in the diocese of Kasai. Nevertheless, abandoning all this comfort, in a movement of interior conversion, Abbé Tshinyama packed his suitcases and returned to Africa. I turn now to describing how he works.

When the people take their place in the church, he puts on his alb, as well as a violet (the traditional color of penance) stole. Joining the assembly, Abbé Tshinyama offers an opening prayer and quickly introduces the theme of the readings of the scripture that are to follow. A short homily follows to set the scene for the action that is going to unfold. The following are a sample of the words with which he addresses those assembled:

> What we are going to do now is a prayer of faith, a request for the mercy of God. This is a rite of healing that is going to manifest once again God's compassion for the suffering and the victory of Christ over evil. But the action of God does not nullify the will of man. That will must be converted and remain in the ways of God. The sorcerer should put an end to his nightly comings and goings and leave his hellish circle. Whoever has placed his refuge and his strength in human magic should leave it and, from now on, put all his hope in the Lord.

A song of penance is then intoned. Before the faithful come forward to where the Abbé Tshinyama waits for them, he requires certain things of them. No one may keep on his person a metal object (such as a bracelet, a chain) or any object that impedes direct contact with the earth (such as shoes). The priest takes the same measures. His alb is pulled up to his hips. He holds a cross as well as a lighted candle in his hands, the cross in his left hand, the candle in his right.

Three acolytes hold him up, one to his right, a second to his left and a third behind him. The faithful who solicit healing come forward to where

Abbé Tshinyama stands. They are to hold their arms extended in the form of a cross, their mouths open, their tongues stuck out. The priest then shows the cross to the one who approaches, stretching the hand in which he holds the candle over the faithful. He prays momentarily with each person approaching and then quickly passes the candle over the length of the person's body from behind. Then, with his left hand holding the cross, he pushes the individual to crawl beneath his legs. Helped by two acolytes, the supplicant kneels, drops down on all fours, and passes beneath the spread legs of the priest. Behind the priest the third acolyte lifts the supplicant and anoints him on the face with the oil of the sick.

Sick people leave healed from this rite, some at the very moment, others over time afterward. Many crutches hang on the walls of the choir in the church of Kabwe as vestiges of these liberations. Moral and spiritual healings are even more numerous than physical ones. I myself have been a witness to a certain number of them.

How are we to assess this rite? Many priests are opposed to it and refuse to have anything to do with it. To crawl between the legs of someone seems a fetishlike gesture and unhealthy. But how is one to take into account that anointing someone with oil, saying that he receives the strength of the Spirit, or putting on his tongue a piece of bread as the body of Christ are gestures that participate in the same process and the same logic as symbols? First, it should be noted that this negative reaction may reveal a certain degree of cultural alienation, which has seriously affected many native African priests, essentially those who have spent formation time in Western institutions. Second, the success of Abbé Tshinyama undoubtedly annoys many pastors who have seen their flocks deserting them to go to Tshinyama. Congolese (Zairian) priests have not been vaccinated against clerical jealousy any more than the Pharisees, priests, and scribes who were contemporaries of Jesus.

The people of God, it should be said, have expressed themselves positively on this healing ritual. This is because, it seems to me, they have rediscovered in it their deepest longings and a way to attain their ideals. In Bantu tradition rites of initiation include a passage of the neophyte beneath the legs of the master. In this case it symbolizes a transmission of forces or mimics a "second birth." The meaning, however, is not only positive, as an event I once witnessed shows. I watched an argument between two women in a train station waiting room where people—lacking seats—were sitting on a tile floor. As one woman went from one corner of the room to the other, she stepped over the child of her neighbor. "Why did you do that? Do you want to give your sicknesses to my child?" the child's mother angrily murmured.

Another example shows the positive side of this ambiguous belief system. In our Congolese (Zairian) villages and in the agricultural suburbs of our cities, during the planting season, one encounters at crossroads peanut and pistachio shells and bean pods that have been thrown on the ground to be trampled on and stepped over. People doing so believe, in effect, that those walking over these shells impregnate them with their life forces. These powers are thought to be transmitted through the shells to the seeds that they once enveloped, rendering them resistant to the rigors of the climate and increasing their fertility. The same action is present in the manufacture of certain traditional fetishes. The ashes of a burnt loin string *(mukaya)* of a young virgin is added to make the fetishes more powerful. One can say that the symbolism of stepping over is connected first with a transmission of both benevolent and evil forces and fertility. Then, it can signify the strain that one accepts to be born again, to pass through the *tunnel of purification.*

In Bantu Christian churches the symbolism of these ritual elements and gestures revolves around belief that power passes from the priest to the sick person. Where does this power come from? Recall that a cross and a lighted candle (fire) are held high by the priest. There appears to be present also the power that the celebrant derives from his ordination, which makes the passage between legs a symbolic placing of the supplicant under the rays of power that emanate from the celebrant's entire being. This is symbolized further by the prayer the priest says and the hand he imposes on the supplicant. This is the Bantu interpretation of the event. It seems to me necessary, in addition, that the paschal mystery be underscored as the source of the power if the rite is to be considered fully Christian. The cross—as the symbol of Christ's victory—does symbolize this; the words of the formula should be more explicit in linking the rite to Christ.

The symbolism of purifying fire bathing the body of the supplicant and chasing away the forces of darkness is clear in the lit candle. Passing beneath the priest is perceived not only as the transmission of healing power but also as a symbol of our struggle to be fully converted. The passage certainly manifests the strain of passing through the narrow gate of the gospels. The anointing at the end is a reminder of the sacrament of the sick. It must be admitted that it is not connected organically with the actions that precede it.

It seems to me that we have here a rich—though also controversial—example of inculturating the sacrament of the sick. It accentuates the healing dimension of the sacrament, which has been ratified in our day by the teachings of the church. This is fortunate because the healing dimension was improperly overshadowed by the dualism of strands of medieval and Scholastic theology that elevated the healing of spirit over the healing of the body. In Black Africa and in the Bible the human person is always thought of integrally as body and spirit. To stress the physical healing dimension is not a perversion of the sacrament. The present experience uses the essential elements of the sacrament—the imposition of hands and the prayer of the priest. The anointing is not necessary. And it shows up in the Kananga celebration as an almost superfluous element. But the fact that it is joined to this practice indicates the continuity with the customary practice of various Christian churches.

At least a few critical comments must be made about elaborate physical gestures in the celebration of the sacrament, gestures that seem to me to call too much attention to the miraculous aspects of the experience. As examples of this I would include making ill persons stick out their tongue, extending their arms, removing their shoes, and getting rid of anything metal. When I asked about these requirements, Abbé Tshinyama answered that they dispose the supplicants to abandon themselves to spiritual action. In removing shoes, chains, and bracelets, the person takes care not to dissipate the magnetism that his body emits. I suggested that what was fundamental to the sacrament was the paschal mystery, and that it was not necessary to make bodily magnetism and the natural gift dimension as important as they were in this rite. I was basing myself on the classic insight that a sacrament's "validity" cannot be understood to depend on the personal gifts of the minister. Undoubtedly a preacher can, by his sin and bad example, impede the transmission of grace, and a holy minister assists by creating a favorable atmosphere for the seed to grow. But in the end, the grace of the sacrament comes from the power of the death and resurrection of Christ.

It is not bad that magnetic and natural elements have a part, but they must be regarded as supplementary. And in this sense, it is good that the rush toward Kabwe ended and that other priests without the same natural gifts as Tshinyama have taken up this ritual with the result that the spectacular elements of the experience of Kabwe were diminished. The people were gradually made aware that the sacrament is not a matter of a miraculous remedy for all sickness but a prayer and a sacrament that express the unconditional abandonment of the Christian to the will of God; the sacrament is not pressure on God to realize our desires. Understood this way the experience reveals the journey of faith and is part of our education in the gratuity of grace.

In this inculturated form the sacrament of the sick could doubtlessly attract people and help them understand the central message of the sacrament, which St. James formulated as "the prayer of faith will save the sick" (Jas 5:15).

By way of conclusion, we can say that Abbé Tshinyama provides us with elements of an inculturated, communitarian celebration of the sacrament of the sick among the Bantus. It is full of symbolism for sick people who walk and who can be brought to the church. We can pass over gestures like taking off shoes or removing metal objects as things revolving around natural magnetism and as idiosyncratic for a certain minister and which should be practiced—if at all—only by him. Whether they are proper in this case is a matter for due deliberation and decision by the church. The elements in this celebration as a whole, however, seem to me to be in accord with a significant community celebration of the sacrament. In this I include passing the lighted candle over the body, holding high the cross, leading the sick person between the legs of the celebrant, and finally the anointing given after the sick one has passed through this gate of liberation. The imposition of hands and the prayer of the priest should be made more prominent than they are in the present version of this rich experience.

7

Presbyteral Ordination

The ordained leadership ministry in the Christian church has always been celebrated as the assignment of the one ordained to a socially important function in the church. Such a celebration entails an assembly of the people, the presence of those in authority, and the assignment of insignia pertinent to the exercise of authority. We shall look briefly at such celebrations in the history of the church and then turn to questions surrounding the future of the sacrament in Africa.

EVOLUTION OF THE RITES OF ORDINATION IN CHRISTIANITY

ORDINATION AND JUDAISM

It should not be surprising, since Christianity arose as a sect of Judaism, that it has kept not only traces of its Jewish roots but also important perspectives from that tradition, especially in the symbolic rituals surrounding ordination to the presbyterate. In what concerns the ordination of ministers in the Christian church, both sacerdotal and rabbinical traditions have furnished important elements, namely, anointing and the imposition of hands.[1]

In Judaism, anointing created kings (see the book of Samuel, the book of Kings) and served to indicate that the anointed one was the bearer of an important mission for the people, in particular for the government. Anointing was done particularly by priests or officials of the Temple. When the Temple and its offices were no longer functioning, the function of judges (Nm 11:16-18) and later of rabbis was given by the imposition of hands and a proclamation by the competent authorities. At the time of Joshua, God says to Moses, "Take Joshua, son of Nun, a man in whom is the spirit, and lay your hand upon him" (Nm 27:18). Joshua, although he had been among the elders to whom the spirit of Moses had been given, needed a special mark as a sign of his being chosen to lead the people.

86

Later the *Mishnah* informs us of a ceremony that confers the juridical-religious function of the judges and later of the rabbis ("masters"). The term used, *semikhah*, entails the imposition of hands and means "to help with the hand." Later, another term, *minui*, meaning "proclamation," is used. As for the Temple priests, they were succeeded by their sons as members of the tribe of Aaron (the Levites); ordination is a different matter altogether. The Temple priests were not the subject of a special choice (except for the ill, who were automatically excluded by Laws of Holiness listed in Leviticus), as is the case in the ordination we are discussing. Because of their office, priests were considered to have the same jurisdiction as rabbis, especially in the interpretation of cultural laws. In fact, their authority was taken over by the Sanhedrin.

However that may be, when Christian rites began to take form, Judaism no longer had the Temple, and the rites from which the Christians could most easily borrow were those for installing rabbis. In this connection two practices seemed to have eventuated. First, the imposition of hands was central. Second, there was the conferral of the title (the proclamation, *minui*). The title was originally given by the master responsible for initiating a disciple whom he judged worthy of succeeding him. Thus the master imposed hands on the candidate and proclaimed him "master." Later, however, the authority of a single master was not considered sufficient, and it was necessary to go through the Sanhedrin or through the head of the council of this Sanhedrin, known as the *Nassi*. The latter officially ordained the rabbi without having to consult the Sanhedrin. The Sanhedrin, however, had always to go through the *Nassi*.

During this ceremony a special vestment adorned with gold (*golta didahaba*) was given. The moral qualities required of an ordinand were wisdom, intelligence, culture, fear of God, physical and moral integrity, masculinity, and Jewish heritage (proselytes were excluded).

THE ORDINATION RITES OF EARLY CHRISTIANITY

The early Christian rites of ordination borrowed the imposition of hands. The Acts of the Apostles already indicates this. The imposition of hands, thus, was applied to the rites of baptism, penance, and the anointing of the sick.

The Greek terms *chirotonie* and *chirothésie* correspond to two juridical connotations. *Chirotonie* was spoken of in connection with bishops, priests, and deacons, while *chirothésie* was applied to lower functions. The gesture of imposition, however, remained the same, although in the East there was an actual imposition of hands, while in the West the gesture was modified to become an extension of the hand toward the ordinand as in the blessing of married couples, evoking the idea of *chirothésie*. In the East all the church offices were conferred with the imposition of hands.[2]

The Latin renders the two Greek terms by *ordinare* ("to set in order"), a term inspired by placing an individual on the Roman *cursus honorum* ("path of honor"). All ecclesiastical functions were conferred by *ordinatio* in the same way a Roman citizen moved upward along the path to higher offices from lower ones. But only the ordination of bishops, priests, and deacons was done by the imposition of hands, according to *The Apostolic Tradition*. Lower offices were conferred with a blessing alone.[3]

FROM HIPPOLYTUS TO THE ANCIENT ROMAN RITE

The period with which we are dealing (roughly from the third to the fifth centuries) had relatively simple rites of ordination. They are divided into three parts and correspond to the three levels of priestly ministry—episcopate, presbyterate, and diaconate. Each of the three rites has the structure and the same major elements: election or call; imposition of hands with a consecratory prayer; and the kiss of peace. There are, however, some differences. The first difference among the three rites consists in the invocations of the consecratory prayer. They specify the grace of the Spirit expected for the discrete function of each office. The second consists in the persons who impose hands. In ordaining bishops, only other bishops impose hands; in ordaining priests, both the bishop and concelebrating priests do so; in ordaining deacons, the bishop alone imposes hands.

In the ancient Roman rite one finds the structure listed by Hippolytus in *The Apostolic Tradition*. However, new symbolic elements pertinent to the functions of the person being ordained are added. In addition, the so-called "minor" orders were increasing (there were already three during this period) and new rites and prayers were composed for them. The lector was blessed after having sworn that he had never succumbed to a grave fault. He was then given the lectionary. The acolyte was blessed after having taken the same precautions, and he was given the utensils of the altar. The subdeacon received the chalice, and he was blessed in the same way as the acolyte.

FRANCO-ROMAN AND FRANCO-GERMAN RITUALS

Between the tenth and the thirteenth centuries, Franco-Roman and Franco-German rituals introduce new elements to the ordination rite. At the ordination of a bishop an anointing of the head is added, as well as rites of investiture such as the enthronement and the bestowal of the cross, miter, and gloves. At the ordination of the priest anointing of the hands, two impositions of hands, and the reception of the chalice are added. At the ordination of the deacon the reception of the Book of the Gospels is added. Minor orders increase in number to five, the two new orders being porter and exorcist. The porter receives a blessing and keys, the exorcist a blessing and the Book of Exorcisms. Clerical tonsure appears without being attached to a minor order and marks entrance into the clerical state before being given access to the different orders. To become a priest, one must climb the ladder of the different orders.

Thus it is in the medieval society that the giving of insignia proper to a function takes on more and more importance in imitation of the secular Roman *cursus honorum*. In this process the principal and appropriately spiritual act of imposing of hands with its accompanying prayer is overshadowed.

EASTERN CHRISTIANITY AND ORDINATION

In the East each of the various churches has its own proper rite, but one finds constants, such as the following: the limitation of lower orders to the subdiaconate and the lectorate; the imposition of hands by a single bishop who presides over the celebration during the ordination of a bishop, while the other concelebrating bishops only touch the head of the ordinand; the ordination to the lower orders with the imposition of hands before the giving of the objects; the imposition of the gospels on the head of the bishop being ordained; the declarative formula of the consecratory prayer: "The divine grace, which always heals the infirm and which supplies for him who lacks, chooses N. as bishop of N. Let us pray, then . . . "

THE CONTEMPORARY ROMAN RITE

The new ritual has revised the prayers of ordination, specifying the task of each order and its proper character. The episcopate is delineated as constituted by the fullness of the sacrament of orders and it affiliates the ordinand with the college of the successors of the apostles. The presbyterate introduces the ordinand into the college of the principal collaborators of the bishop. The diaconate is regarded as not included in the priesthood but as a specific service of the bishop and the Christian community. The minor orders have been suppressed as stages in the old *cursus honorum* pattern. They have been reduced to two and become particular liturgical services. The lectorate appoints an individual to the service of the word, and acolytes are installed to the service of the eucharist. One no longer speaks of the consecration of the bishop but simply of his ordination, thus underlining the unity of the episcopacy with the other two orders—presbyterate and diaconate. The idea of a *cursus* is maintained to the extent that one cannot become a bishop without having passed through the presbyterate, just as one cannot become a presbyter without having been first a deacon. However, one can be ordained and remain a permanent deacon without intending to advance to the presbyterate—thus instituting the status of transitory and permanent deacons to the post–Vatican II church.

The structure of the three rites remains the same as in *The Apostolic Tradition* of Hippolytus of Rome: (1) the "call," involving a presentation of candidates, election or reading of the papal letter or allocution, prayer of the community (litanies), during which the candidate prostrates; (2) the essential rite involving an imposition of hands and a prayer of consecration; (3) the insignia and explanatory rites, including the anointings (on the head for the bishop, on the hands only for the priest), conferral of priestly or diaconal vestments and the insignia of the bishop, such as laying the Book of the Gospels on the head, handing over the crosier and miter, and installing the bishop in his *cathedra*; and finally (4) the kiss of peace, which closes the rite.

TOWARD AN APPROPRIATE AFRICAN CELEBRATION OF THE SACRAMENT

THE PRIEST IN THE CHURCHES OF BLACK AFRICA

The customs of the colonial era, with its separation of expatriates from local people, set the missionary priest apart from the people. That carried over into the structures that are generally in place when a Black African priest takes over the role of the foreign missionary. He is effectively separated from the mass of his people, living in an elevated social status. He is almost always seen as the "new Bwana" (literally, "the new chief,") and he becomes a kind of "new white man."

It is a fact that an African who became a priest in colonial society was often the "flower" of the flock. Seminaries—despite the intentions of their administrators—were schools that in country after country provided political leaders at the time of independence. Still, the fact that the indigenous priest was obliged to the law of celibacy removed him from the function of bestowing life for his people and in an important sense made the priest an unfortunate in regard to his clan. That remains a disconcerting element in African Catholic churches despite efforts to reinterpret the tradition for the people to help them esteem religious celibacy lived in the service of love as a love that constitutes a sort of a new fertility.[4]

What qualities do Africans expect of a priest? We can group them as follows:

- a priest should be an adult and an initiate—an adult in his way of understanding things, in his relationships with people and society, a man capable of assuming his responsibilities, a man who knows interior realities;
- a priest should live close to the people; priesthood has nothing to do with being a "parachutist" in the church; he is not a functionary named by a distant administrator;
- a priest is "consecrated," a man of God, a man who reflects

transcendence and who calls others to communion with the spiritual dimension, a spiritually powerful person whose life constitutes a channel of transmission between the ordinary world and the world of transcendence beyond;

- a priest is an elder, someone who takes the lead, who offers himself to defend others, one who intercedes, who kindles and rekindles the fire of the hearth; he is, in other words, a kind of chief.

If these are the expectations, the symbols that are proposed for the ordination rite ought to correspond to them. The gestures and symbols proposed in the African rituals of ordination are borrowed from two traditions—enthronement and initiation. Let us consider enthronement first, because the functions of sanctifying, governing, and teaching are preeminently functions of a chief. In African cultures the traditional chief is not the summit of a hierarchy. He is, instead, a man endowed with a power that opens him to the supernatural so that the power of the Transcendent can direct the human community. It was natural, then, for our faithful to understand this priestly function as the conferral of spiritual power. Ordination in Cameroon is a clear example of this. The new priest is carried in a kind of wickerwork throne made of palm branches, and flour and millet (characterizing fertility and abundance) are thrown in his path.[5]

The second tradition is that of initiation. In effect, to become a channel of transmission between the ordinary world and the world of transcendence demands an initiation. Thus it is with healers, chiefs, and professions that involve manipulating powers of the universe. Among gestures of initiation is the touching of the foreheads of the initiator and the one initiated. In the perspective of initiation, prostration is interpreted as a symbolic mimicry of death; putting on new clothes as a stepping across a new threshold; and anointing with lime by the elders or parents as a sign of harmonization in the communion of life. The word of the parents is asked for in the first part of the rite, after the call. The parents of the ordinand are asked for their ratification of the step their son is embarked on. They give lime to their son to manifest not only their agreement but also their union with the act that will be done.

An Ordination Rite from Kasai

The ordination ritual from Kasai[6] is organized with a number of traditional elements in the first part of the ceremony. They center around the call of those to be ordained.

First, a priest calls the ordinands by name. They individually respond, "Here I am," and move toward the bishop. Their parents are at their side as they walk toward the bishop, who asks if the ordinands are worthy. The priest who presents them responds:

According to the opinion of those who have followed their formation, we believe they are worthy. But their parents are here. Let us
hear from them about this matter.

The bishop turns toward the parents and asks if they wish to speak
and if they give their children freely and with all their heart. They express
themselves, manifesting their joy at their sons' decisions, declaring their
commitment to them and demanding that the church take good care of
them. Here is an example of a parent's remarks about his son:

This man . . . is our flesh and blood. His commitment is also our
own. We give him wholeheartedly to the church. We will stand by
him. But watch him well, assure him good conditions for work.
Surround him with affection and solicitude. We have done our work.
It is up to you to do yours now.

Turning toward their son, the parents give him the white kaolin, saying to him:

The insect that destroys the bean is inside it. We who brought you
into the world have never betrayed you. We will continue to struggle
at your side. Here is the lime; we are with you.

They put a little white kaolin on his forehead. The bishop concludes
the first part of the liturgy by saying, "We choose you for the order of
priest," and the assembly applauds.

When the call is finished, the rest of the rite follows the Roman ritual
until the kiss of peace. At that point the bishop places his hands on the
temples of the new priest and then touches his forehead to the ordinand's,
saying, "Be strong as the *muswaswa*, as the hammer and the anvil" [a
formula for wishing vitality to another]. The concelebrating priests do
the same.

In the ordination of deacons we note in the diocese of Kole in Congo
(Zaire) the ritual act of stepping over a white line traced on the ground to
signify commitment. This comes from the rite of Osidji, where the com-
batant who crosses the line commits himself to persevere all the way to
victory. In Mbujimayi, once, instead of giving the Book of the Gospels to
the prospective deacons, the book was placed on the ground and those
being ordained stepped over it, reminding the ordinands of the traditional gestures when a solemn oath is given and powers are transmitted.

Much more could be said about the inculturation of the rite of the
sacrament of orders for Africa. These few pages at least raise the question and give some idea how the church in the Congo (Zaire) is facing the
issue.

8

Blessings and Consecrations

CHRISTIAN TRADITIONS SURROUNDING BLESSINGS AND CONSECRATIONS

The history of religions teaches that the notion of the *sacred* is common to all religions. For all customs, space is not homogeneous; there are ruptures in the levels where the "divine" springs forth into the "terrestrial."[1] These spaces where the divine irrupts become the object of rites performed by humans in order to tap this power for profane use and to mark this rupture in the ordinary. Sacred places can be waters, lands, valleys, buttes, grottos, certain trees, and objects.

In this perspective we find such places as Bethel, Gilgal, Sinai, and the Temple in Israelite religion, in addition to such things as the ark, cups and chandeliers, vestments for worship, rites of purification and consecration, the Sabbath, and the cycle of liturgical feasts that historicize sacred encounters. What is original in relation to other religions is that Judaism eventually came to hold that only Yahweh, the Holy One, could create a truly sacred event, thing, or place. Yahweh's proximity and power alone sanctified and consecrated. The Christian scriptures tap into this vein.

The apostles of Jesus continue Jewish blessings over the meal (see Mt 14:19) and blessings of persons (see Mk 21:23-24; Lk 24:26-50). But Jesus emphasizes the fundamental reality that it is the gift of God that consecrates and sanctifies. Over time St. Paul will stipulate that the ultimate blessing is to receive the gift of the Holy Spirit, which makes us God's adopted children (see Eph 1:3-5; 4).

The theology of the twelfth century distinguished between consecrations and blessings. The best illustration of this can be found in the letter of Gilbert, bishop of Limerick:

I would speak of "blessing" as far as it concerns objects that are not used during the offices of the church. For that which would be used

93

as instruments for cult, I would say "consecrate." The pontiff blesses the queen, the virgin when she takes the veil, or any of the faithful who come to him for his blessing. . . . It is the bishop who consecrates objects of cult, such as the vestments or liturgical ornaments of the priest or bishop, or the linens on the altar, chalice, paten, corporal, ciborium, chrisma . . . in sum, all that is separated from profane usage and reserved for the divine cult.[2]

But the liturgy did not retain these distinctions, and over time we see overlapping, where the same rites are referred to sometimes as consecrations and sometimes as blessings. Consecrations tend toward the officially sacramental, while blessings mostly remain in the domain of actions that are simply meant to help the faithful find sanctification in ordinary things and the progress of their spiritual life. What does not pertain to the official sacraments will eventually be identified as the "sacramentals."

However valuable these distinctions are, in dealing with the experience of the church in Africa, we must not limit ourselves to these categories. This will block the natural blossoming of new liturgical perspectives in Black Africa. What seems to me fundamental and to be emphasized is the fundamental Christian notion of blessing.[3] This is the center and point of convergence for other hints of the nature of the sacred.

Please recall that the expression "Bless God" is the most frequently used expression using the word *blessing* in the Bible. The Hebrew word *berek* means "to bend one's knees" (see Dn 6:11; Ps 95 [94]:6), to adore, praise, and invoke God's name (see Ex 18:10; 2 Sm 18:28; Ps 16:7). To bless a man or a thing is to invoke the favor of God upon it. God is the source of blessing. God alone can bless. God blessed created things after making them (Gn 1:22ff.); God blessed Noah (Gn 9:1), Abraham and the Patriarchs (Gn 27:16), and those things that served the realization of the divine plan, for example, the Sabbath (Gn 2:3), bread and wine (Ex 23:25), the work of Job (Jb 1:10). When humans bless, they are imitating God. For human beings, "to bless" is to call on God, to invoke God to come upon what the human being blesses. Melchizedek blessed Abraham in this fashion (Gn 14:19), Naomi blessed Boaz (Ru 2:20), fathers blessed their infants (Gn 28: 4-7,10), priests blessed the people (Nm 6:22-27; Lv 9:22-23), and Moses blessed the tribes of Israel (Dt 33:1) by invoking on them the graces of God. In sum, the originality of Jewish and Christian blessing consists in invoking the name of God.

BLESSING IN BLACK AFRICAN TRADITIONS

The Black African world is conceived as dual—part visible and part invisible—but coherent, not dualism in the sense of a chasm between the spiritual and the physical. The two faces of being are united by the same energy—life. All beings on earth and in heaven participate in this energy to varying degrees. The invisible world is both transcendent and imma-nent. This is why beings from both dimensions of reality can influence beings in the other. All subordinate beings turn to the Supreme Being as their last resort. And before that occurs, they will have turned first to their ancestors and to non-incarnate, benevolent spirits.[4]

Humans are in their very being considered a wish for life, a vehement desire to live, a movement, a march, "a grain that is in the process of becoming a *baobab*," that is to say, a life force sustained by God. Hu-mans are a miniature cosmos, an intersection or relay in the exchange of life force. We integrate and cooperate with all other earthly elements in the struggle for victory in life. We can talk to the plants and animals, to the rocks and stars. We can even enter into the being of others—whether animals or plants—to save or to hurt someone.[5]

Black African traditions are hostile to the systematic separation of sacred and profane, seeing them as two faces of the same reality. The sacred is part of the everyday, but it is not confused with the everyday. It is the same with humans and the world, the below and the above, the body and the spirit. All "copenetrate" without confusion. And so it is that all life is impregnated with the rhythm of the creator and remains in harmony with both the visible and invisible universe. The black African is predisposed to see through the visible as an irruption of the invisible. And therefore one finds places, objects, and moments reserved for that irruption from above to occur.

For the black African, to bless is to harmonize our being with the rhythm of the world and of God. It is to dispose the natural forces in favor of life, to eliminate the evil in one's heart, to disperse bad spirits and honor the ancestors. Thus the blessing of the black African consists of purifications, deliverances, conjuring away bad spells, preventing pos-sible assailants from wreaking harm. Above all, blessings are acts of harmonization and wishes for happiness and prosperity.

THE ENCOUNTER OF CHRISTIAN
AND AFRICAN NOTIONS OF BLESSING

Both Christian and African blessings consist principally of calling the favors of the supernatural onto the individual in this world. In Africa, even if the supernatural is protected by God, the Christian African must make God's role explicit and recenter all blessings around salvation in Jesus Christ. Concretely, Africans take the symbols and signs of blessing in their traditions and use them to participate in the harmony brought by Jesus Christ through his death and resurrection. In this way the blessing brings a life whose plenitude is in addition to and beyond the legacy of the ancestors. The African Christian does not take a detour or reject traditions; rather, he or she corrects their trajectories. The rites that we describe below are living demonstrations of how that correction is made, when Christ and the history of salvation become the "pole of harmonization" in a world that continues to be understood as dual and marked by diverse participations and mediations shared by ancestors, human beings, animals, vegetables, and seemingly inanimate objects.

AFRICAN RELIGIOUS CONSECRATIONS

Of all of the inculturated rites in Africa, it seems to me that the consecration of a religious is the one most boldly conceived. I have already written on this subject elsewhere.[6] The first example for our discussion is from Cameroon.

The rite for profession in the Congregation of the Beatitudes, founded by Father Engelbert M'veng[7] and Sister Therese Michele in Cameroon, is original. The family of the prospective religious steps toward the altar and presents their daughter (or son), completely giving her up. Then they offer her a stalk of the palm tree and say, "Be like a palm whose fruit gives precious oil. In your consecration, be productive."

She is then presented with a stalk of *makabo,* a plant with large leaves whose configuration allows rain water to run down their own stalks as well as those of their neighbors. Words commending solidarity and support are spoken, and the candidate responds, "Thank God."

The celebrant then questions the candidate, "Do you remember if you have anything against your brother or sister?" The candidate asks the forgiveness of all. She prostrates herself during the singing of the litanies. The celebrant concludes with a formula of absolution, and the call, the invitation, and the profession of the vows are made. The formula is rooted in the beatitudes and is intended to send them on to their mission. A portion follows:

> Lord Jesus, you who said, "Happy are the poor, the Kingdom of heaven is theirs," I promise on your tomb and on your resurrection to consecrate to you my whole life and to live as you lived in the family of Nazareth a life of evangelical poverty, of consecrated celibacy, a life of planned community, a life as a messenger of the gospel, ready to announce the good news wherever your Holy Spirit and our Mother the Holy Church send me, without fear of man and not presumptuous of my strengths, conforming to the order of life of the Family of the Beatitudes. In the name of the Father, Son, and Holy Spirit.

The candidate then receives a ring and a cross.

The Monastery of the Poor Clares of Lilongwe in Malawi uses corn flour (the symbol of life, *Nsima;* the staple in the diet of the people is made from corn flour) to express the gift given on the part of the parents. They offer flour to the celebrant as a sign that they are offering the life of their child. Religious also use fire as a symbol of their contribution and their cooperation in the work of the consecration of their sister. In a way similar to initiation, one of the responsible parties or a superior rubs oil on the candidate. In traditional rituals the one who gives the name to the child is the one who rubs this oil.

In Congo (Zaire) the rites of religious profession have three elements: inviting the involvement of the parents and the ancestors; offering a pact of blood; and performing the rites of initiation. In Kinshasa the rite of the pact of blood is the central part of the ceremony. The words of the celebrant follow:

> You are now going to offer a drop of your blood on this white cloth. This cloth stained with your pure blood will be placed next to the rock of the altar and will remain there. It symbolizes the offering of your life every day in the service of the glory of God, our Father, and of men and women, our brothers and sisters. At the moment of communion, Christ will give you his blood, most holy and pure. You will drink it. And so, the pact of friendship between you and Christ will be concluded.

When this is said, one by one the candidates prick their fingers to draw blood. They touch the cloth, which has been placed on the knees of the bishop. Next, the master of ceremonies presents the cloth to the faithful. The bishop then stands, turns to the people, and recites the prayer of blessing. Afterwards, the master of ceremonies places the now-stained cloth next to the stone of the altar.

The profession rite of the Sisters of Charity places a great deal of emphasis on the parents and elders and through them on the ancestors. The rite begins with a dialogue between the parents and the bishop concerning their frame of mind about their daughter. This dialog is extended to the entire community in a traditional form of discourse. Before reciting the formula for her commitment, the candidate receives the blessing of her parents. In Kasai this blessing is done with white kaolin or with the ashes from their home hearth. The parents say:

> We who are your family, we have nothing against you, we let you leave, without rancor, may your way be white like the kaolin. Do not step on the scorpion or the snake. May you only find soft earth beneath your feet.

At Matadi in lower Congo (Zaire), the blessing of parents takes place with a cola nut, palm wine, a movement of the arms upward, and the words of an uncle or aunt. He (or she) invokes the Supreme Being and then the line of the ancestors. Then he chews a cola nut, sips palm wine, takes this mixture and spits it onto the hands and arms of the candidate. Then he lifts up the candidate's arms three times and states his wish for a life that is strong, fruitful, and persevering, saying, "*Sambuka, kinda, siama.*" The candidate responds, "*Yobo*" (May it be that way).

The Mothers of Bethany[8] also give the parents a prominent place in the profession ritual and add the pact of blood at the communion. Their original element consists in the presentation of three symbols at the moment of profession using the following formula:

> In the name of the Father, the Son, and the Holy Spirit. Before you, our Bishop, N., I, N., in complete freedom of spirit and of heart bind myself by oath to God and to the Holy Virgin Mary. I promise to raise my heart from things of this earth (and she shows a pearl necklace). I promise to keep my linens private in saving myself alone for the Lord—he holding the leopard, and me, holding the banana tree (she shows a bouquet of banana leaves lashed with white fabric). I promise to dispose my heart to obey, like a goat that never refuses its master's leash, no matter how rough it is (she shows a piece of rope), according to the rule of the Mothers of Bethany, this oath having been made this (day, month, year).

The ritual of Mbandaka adds a few elements. While the religious makes her profession, she holds in her hands a cord of raffia. As each vow is pronounced, she ties a knot in the cord, and when she finishes the three vows she has three knots. The cord will be reserved in a sacred place. As an emblem, the bishop places a hoop bracelet made of ivory on the wrist of the religious. After the eucharist the family waits for the newly consecrated at the door of the church. There a dance of initiation begins. Around her neck they place horns, and in her right hand they put a special machete and in her left hand a lance. The skin of a totem animal or of a monkey that is reputed to be very strong is tied around her hips. She jumps with this "armor" and makes a tour around the court. She reenters the church as the crowd applauds. We find the same special machete in the profession ceremony of the congregation of the Sons of God at Luiza. It is a symbol of initiation and maturity. This weapon or tool is given to the newly professed as the conclusion of the ceremony.

The important moments determined by the Roman ritual for religious profession can all be found in the rites described above—the call and interrogation, profession of the vows, admonition, the prayer of the celebrant and the assembly, and finally, the giving of an emblem. But these different elements are highlighted in distinctive ways by the groups who celebrate these African profession rituals.

BLESSING A CHRISTIAN WIDOW (OR WIDOWER)

In Bantu tradition a widow mourns her husband at least one year. The first week of this mourning is particularly severe. The widow stays silent within her house. Her only words are the traditional hymn to the dead and the recitation of the family's genealogy. She eats only what is given to her. That nourishment is very meager, and it is served on the bark of a tree or on a shard of pottery. She does not bathe; she can only go to the toilets if she pays a fine, and then only during the night when no one can see her. Sometimes she is struck by her sisters-in-law under the pretext that she somehow caused the death of their brother. In addition, she may wear only rags during this week. From the moment of the death of her spouse, she wears a white cloth called the *mukaya* (a special kind of slip) as a sign that she is quarantined from the community and is in communion with the deceased.

These rituals of mourning for the widow have been changing in Africa because of the demands of life in the cities, but the same is true also in Christian communities in the villages. Christian morality has challenged some of these practices. Nonetheless, certain African perspectives on how widows are to behave cannot be considered offensive to the life of faith in Jesus Christ. In Christian communities we ensure that the widow is no longer struck or deprived of nourishment. She is surrounded by friends or by Christian neighbors, who make sure no harm comes to her. She will still wear under her other clothes a piece of white linen as a sign of being placed in quarantine. Instead of holding a powerful herb to fend off malevolent spirits, she holds a cross surrounded by flowers. She abstains from bathing herself during the first week as a sign of her sadness. In urban settings the period of mourning is usually shortened to two or three days for the broader assembly of mourners, but the close family still observes a seven-day period, sometimes longer.

After all this is done and everyone has left, the widow returns to ordinary life while maintaining her bereavement. She takes up everyday work but refrains from participating in money-making or public activities. She does not wear gaudy clothing but maintains a quiet modesty in her dress. Some widows wear white clothing, which is the traditional color for mourning in Africa, while others wear black, a sign that they have been Europeanized.

After the entire period of mourning is over (one year at least), the widow prepares a great feast, inviting as many people as she can afford. In urban settings the ending of the period of mourning brings financial gain, since the invited guests each bring a sum of money to the widow, according to their status. The feast is not huge, but it is a hearty meal to which the family of her late husband is invited. The brother-in-law whom she has chosen as her new husband does not attend. Rather, they will meet at a crossroad of the village during the night for a ritual act of coitus that breaks the carnal bond with the late husband. In cities, well before the solemn feast that lifts the mourning period, the widow will have organized a private meal with the family and the rite that follows the ritual coitus. It is sometimes difficult to find a brother or close relative of the dead husband in the city. In such a case the widow searches for someone from the same village or tribe as the deceased, and the location for the ritual act of coitus moves from the crossroads to a garden or under a tree.

The first transformation of this ritual on the part of Christianity was to protect the widow from harmful actions by her husband's family. These harmful actions—easily viewed as contrary to the Christian faith and the law of charity—must, however, be understood in context. They functioned as an escape valve to release the tension and upset caused by the husband's death by making the wife a scapegoat. The use of the cross and the flowers that are placed in the hands of the widow constitute another change. The prayers recited, as well as the songs sung, which underline the victory of Christ over death, balance the traditional funerary hymns.

The practice of the private dinner for the family of the deceased and of the ritual act of coitus continues. There has been an effort by the Christian community to prohibit this ritual. No meaningful alternative has been proposed, however, and that leaves a hole in the observance of a death, an incompleteness for which a substitute must be found. After some research, we have found new developments to mark the end of the period of mourning that address this need.

In rural communities around Cijiba in Kasai, when the day for lifting the solemn period of mourning for the Christian widow comes, the community walks in procession to the cemetery. In prayer, the community accompanies the widow to the tomb of her husband. The priest and acolytes, in liturgical garb, carry a cross in plain view, as well as a thurible, holy water, and a bible. They are followed by the widow, who wears new clothes. The procession leaves the church, walking to the sounds of a song that recalls the compassion of God and God's providence. Arriving at the tomb, they encircle it and the priest incenses the area. He introduces the rite with an invitation to pray for the deceased and the widow. There is a reading evoking the compassion and consolation of God or the joy of the Christian (Phil 4:4-9), followed by a psalm (Ps 90), after which the priest reads the gospel of the sending of the disciples (Mt 10: 7-12) or the mission of Christ (Lk 4:18). He then comments on the reading, if circumstances permit, perhaps saying, for instance, that the widow is called to witness to Christ, thus clearing the path to the Kingdom.

To signify in a sensible and striking manner the rupture of the matrimonial bond, we have experimented with another gesture—placing the
wedding band on the grave while the widow speaks solemnly (she may
use any object that recalls their married life). She places the ring on the
grave, saying:

> You, N., my husband, know the love that united us and that unites
> us still. I know that from where you are, you want me to live and
> not to die of sorrow. I have spent a year feeling my pain and crying
> for you. It is time for me to stand up and continue the journey that
> we started together. I have come to solemnly say goodbye and to
> give you the ring that bound me physically and morally to you. I
> ask that you help me find someone else, if necessary, another com-
> panion on the way, so that life may continue.

She places the ring on the tomb and she sprinkles it with holy water in
the sign of the cross. Then she turns her back on the tomb and begins to
walk home. The acolyte, carrying the large cross, walks before her. The
priest invites the assembly to prayer. With his hand pointing toward the
woman, he says,

> Lord, you who gave N. (the name of deceased husband) to N. (name
> of widow), you have taken him to your arms. Give to N. the cour-
> age to continue to fight for life in this world and to prepare herself
> for happiness in heaven. May sadness not overwhelm her. May her
> trials not cripple her so that she may be a witness to the joy of one
> who is called by you to live in you and for you. Take away evil
> impediments. Keep her far away from bad friends, for after having
> endured this test, may she not sink into the trap of deception and
> treason. Give her the joy of hope in your presence, you who are
> God, compassionate, tender, and full of pity. We ask you this
> through our Lord Jesus Christ, your son, and our Lord. Amen.

The priest then incenses the direction where the widow has turned and
the choir sings a song about sending someone on a mission or a psalm
that expresses confidence in God. The procession returns to the church,
the cross in advance, followed by the widow and the faithful, the priest,
and the acolytes. Once they have gathered in the church, the liturgy moves
directly to the offerings that are made by the widow. Things such as
chicken, tea, coffee, drinks, and flour that are part of the offering are for
the family of the deceased and for the poor. This connects the Christian
celebration to the traditional meal prepared by the widow for the family
of the deceased one. Mass is celebrated for the deceased.

If it is not possible for the widow and the community to pray at the
cemetery for reasons of distance or weather, the entire rite can take place

in the church after the homily. Songs of penitence are sung, and friends accompany the widow to the altar. She places the wedding band or precious object in a basket at the foot of the altar and speaks to her husband as she would have at the grave. The priest blesses the ring and the community sings of Christian mission as she returns to her seat. The ring and the offerings of food will be given to the poor by the parish community. If the person celebrating the end of the period of mourning is a widower, the ritual remains the same, making any adaptations necessary in the prayers.

BLESSING OF FIELDS AND PLANTING NEW CROPS

Work in the fields occupies a great deal of the population of Black Africa. It is work that is tied to survival. There are numerous traditional African rites that revolve around the agricultural life of the community and that are intended to ensure its success. These rites essentially consist of an effort to separate the fields and the planting season from any problems that could cause infertility and any division that would bring death. We have said that for the Christian to bless a thing, a person, or an activity is to call the grace of God upon it by pronouncing the name of Jesus Christ and invoking the grace and power of his salvation. When the Christian community turns to the question of blessing the harvest, it becomes necessary to keep the focus on the ultimate human good—staying open to the grace of God and human destiny—so that all other goods and needs are kept in relation to this final destiny. The following is a ritual blessing that adheres to this principle.

The faithful bring a small amount of soil from their fields and some seeds destined for planting to the church. The priest, vested in liturgical garb, stands at the church entrance with an acolyte carrying holy water. Songs and introductory words recall the truth that "without the Lord we can do nothing, and nothing can be fruitful." The priest invites the faithful to deposit the soil in one pot and the seeds in another. The priest blesses the earth, asking that it be protected so that no accidents, dangers, thorns, or injuries from tools may occur in the fields. He then blesses the seeds, asking that they produce a hundredfold. Then he sprinkles holy water over them, asking that there be plentiful rains and good sunshine. The procession then moves inside the church, where the two pots are placed at the foot of the altar. Psalm 50 is sung and then the sign of peace is exchanged. Readings follow and mass continues as usual.

As we look at this rite of blessing for a good harvest, we see that the animist conception of the world is united with the Christian. To bring soil from one's fields is to have brought the entire field; to take even one grain from among the seeds for planting is to have brought all of one's planting stock to the altar. But it is God who germinates the seeds, who makes things grow, and who produces a bountiful harvest. The word of God read at this occasion will serve to underscore that truth (Gn 1:27-31; Ps 125; Jn 12:23-26).

BLESSING THE SEASON OF CATERPILLARS

During the month of February in Kasai caterpillars are collected in the wooded savanna. This period is not without danger, and many deaths of young people occur because they lack experience and fail to protect themselves from the venomous snakes that are present. The caterpillar nourishes. But it also symbolizes the change of life, conversion, a new birth. In fact, the caterpillar becomes the butterfly. From caterpillar to butterfly a total change has taken place. The following is a celebration for the beginning of this season that we have put together during a eucharist: (1) an entrance song, calling for conversion; (2) readings that recall the fruits of the Easter of the Lord and the transformation of the first Christians (Acts 2:37-47) and the signs of the times (Lk 21:29-33); (3) a homily that focuses on the phenomenon of the caterpillars being transformed into butterflies, which underlines the possibility of Christian conversion; (4) a prayer of the faithful; (5) a blessing of the season, during which a branch with several caterpillars on it is placed in front of the altar and sprinkled with holy water while a prayer asks for a multitude of caterpillars and for the protection of all who will be gathering them (the priest turns toward the people and blesses them, invoking the glory of God upon them and imploring for them the grace of a permanent conversion); and (6) offerings are made and the eucharist follows.

It seems to me that if we follow a rite such as the one described above, we are allowing African Christians to celebrate the different times and seasons of their culture. And there are many such celebrations, such as the dry season, the rainy season, the new moon, the season of harvests, and so on. Thus the entirety of life is brought under the aegis of the gospel's teaching that all we are and do is known to God and of concern to God.

BLESSING BEWITCHED INFANTS

This ritual presupposes that one recognizes that sorcery is a social reality in Black Africa. It is motivated by the desire of one person or group to harm the life of another by witchcraft.[9] Often infants are introduced into the chain of witchcraft by malevolent adults. Therefore, finding a way to rid them of witchcraft is necessary for pastoral practice and of great concern to ordinary people. This is done in a ritual comprised of five parts: (1) a call and interrogation of affected parties about what they have done and what they desire; (2) a supplication and blessing with holy water, during which the interested parties prostrate themselves before the altar while Psalm 50 is sung; the priest blesses them with holy water and invokes the grace of baptism; (3) cutting of the hair (a traditional rite of deliverance) by the priest to implore the grace that keeps the evil from returning and reinforces the desire for good; (4) a cry of solidarity against the evil (also a traditional rite during the process of deliverance), during which the assembly is invited to cry out against the evil and to invoke curses while the affected parties stand; and (5) prayer and the imposition of hands by the priest; a prayer is said that recalls the liberating mission of Christ (Lk 4:18-19).

It is hard to overstate the importance of such blessings for the education of the Christian people, for bringing to them a tangible sense of the protection of God against the powers of evil, and for actually accomplishing the vanquishment of these powers. In devising such rituals the African church is following the path of Celtic, Frankish, and other branches of Christianity in attempting to make practical and apparent the blessings of Christian life and its role in practical, everyday reality.

9

What Society? Which Church? Whose Theology?

SACRED RITES AND SOCIAL CHANGES

The more I ponder the question of rites and social change and relations, the more I realize that they resemble an iceberg; only one-tenth can be observed, and nine-tenths lies below our line of sight. Many changes in the rituals we have been discussing did not happen by chance. They are in fact very much linked with the entire *project* of postcolonial societies, a word that deserves italics to invoke the fact that our attempts to steer the course of the ship called "church" in the midst of broad social change is full of imponderables. The pastor of the parish of St. Joseph of Liberty (Tshikapa-Kele), where the first experiment with reading ancestral wisdom during the eucharist took place, wrote the following:

The impact produced is much more profound than many thought it would be. It regards conscious social change and involves an alteration of speech and practices that "enslave" many people around the world even today—speech patterns and practices surrounded by taboos and myths guarding people in the midst of changes in overwhelming structures whose main features once normalized and guided both thought and practices. The 1982 Tshikapa experiment, which has in the last two years entered a decisive phase, . . . focuses attention on enduring methods of thinking about our peoples' relationship to money, sex, and cultures. . . . In brief, it is about our gathering as social, historical, free societies in the face of enduring socially constructed structures both of domination and ways to escape domination and freely to construct alternative, new structures. Hence, it is not an easy, merely "adventuresome" task that we can establish on outdated speech patterns that are clearly racist and devoid of deeper analyses and weighing of our social situation.[1]

We have seen the beginning of a social change in small local communities where the people slowly are attributing the African titles to Jesus. Once people begin to attribute to Christ traditional titles like chief, hero, rock of refuge, rainbow, or the shield that breaks the spear, they begin to understand the true connotation of these titles. In Christ they find an incomparable richness mediated by these titles, and this new consciousness leads them to modify their understanding of both Christ and the titles.[2] These titles—when reapplied to chiefs and cultural heroes—can make the people critical toward their leaders, whom they see enjoying these titles without meriting them. People understand, in other words, that their elders and chiefs are not models of power and leadership and that Christ alone is the true model.

RITES AND THE PATH TO REALIZING A CHURCH THAT IS FAMILY

In the African cultures of yesterday, as in those of today, family is a very important reality because this small-scale society is built upon a covenant, communion, and solidarity. It is true that Black African cities have today made necessary new networks of relationships—commercial relations, relations among neighbors, and a new relationship due to complex religious interaction. What is most interesting to note in these new relations is that they are all patterned after the model of the family. It is as if through these new networks we Africans have been working tirelessly to retain our family spirit. For example, one will find in the working place the presence of elders (who are considered to be elder brothers and sisters), youngsters (who are like younger brothers and sisters), fathers, mothers, and children, depending on the nature of the job, which may concentrate an age-group cohort to work in the same place or office. It is not by chance that in our Christian communities the responsible people are called elders and that one does not address such a person as Mr. or Mrs. but as Papa or Mama. In the majority of Christian communities the diocesan priest is addressed as papa, chief or Abbé.

Some of the major attempts to integrate the family analogy into the heart of the African church appear in the rites and the celebrations we have been discussing. The example of Pastor Willy Mnyagwata in Zimbabwe is noteworthy. He once invited the elder brothers of two enemies in a Christian community to a Christian reconciliatory rite. As we have already noted, all African eucharistic prayers mention the ancestors and either invoke or relate the prayers of the community to them. As we have also seen, the profession of religious, marriages, and priestly ordinations give a very important role to the family of those concerned.[3]

In this context it seems to me worth recalling that the concept of church as family, manifested in rituals, calls for a specific way of life on the part of priests who are responsible for Black African Christian communities. We have seen how the rite of ordination considers the priest as an elder and as a chief, which are two important responsibilities in our cultures.

An elder or a chief without a family is unthinkable in our cultures because he must be like the ancestors—a symbol of the transmission of life. Since the symbol unifies in itself the life visible and invisible, it is not enough that a priest exhibit only spiritual fatherhood (i.e., invisible life). In the concept of church as family in Black Africa, priests and the bishops responsible to and for local Christian community must also be married and fathers of families. If the pastor is a person who has not transmitted life, he will be considered like a functionary who comes to a particular place for a certain period of time to perform a certain job. Even more, he will be considered as a kind of child, not as a full adult. It is enough to see how celibates are looked upon and treated in African traditions. No matter what their chronological age, they will never be able to sit in a meeting where the problems of life are treated. Marital experience is considered a requisite if a man is to exercise responsibility for guiding the human community.

No doubt there are African traditions where sexual continence is demanded. There is a requirement of virginity for women, for instance, before marriage among certain groups. Continence is required on the vigils of solemn visits of chiefs or warriors and for six months for the individual who supplies milk to the king.[4] But this kind of "celibacy" is always for a stipulated period of time, such as for the duration of a particular celebration. It is never viewed as a permanent state of life. In certain African initiations the experience of human sexuality is evoked to stimulate communion with the creator and solidarity with the ancestors. It is significant that a dead individual without progeny is excluded from the list of Bantu ancestors.

This does not mean that consecrated celibacy is condemned in Africa. We have already mentioned that in certain African traditions it is thought necessary to abstain from sexual relations and even from ordinary common activities to prepare oneself better for certain important events, such as war, undertaking an important journey, or preparing for an important meeting. Vowed religious in Africa are also considered to be people set apart for the triumph of the Kingdom of God. But it is also *not* their role to govern Christian communities. According to our cultural norms, the role of the head or of the elder of a community should be exercised by married priests or bishops. Here we are different from Orthodox traditions, in which episcopacy is largely reserved to followers of monastic life. This kind of celibacy is not an integral part of the sacred order received from the Lord, even if its evolution in the West is a venerable and holy tradition.

In the African understanding of the world, a person responsible for the community shares completely the life of the members. In this perspective religious-priests (i.e., members of religious orders such as Jesuits or Dominicans) are people set apart exclusively for the Kingdom of God and should not be priests in charge of parishes. They can only be animators of certain celebrations to which they are called in as visitors or when they are called upon to accomplish specific duties at a particular moment in a Christian community.

In advancing this discussion here, I am not seeking to dislodge or discomfort the many faithful African diocesan priests who are celibates because of the *de facto* structure of ministerial priesthood in the Catholic church. They attempt to follow their commitment with fidelity, believing that their celibacy results from a decision of faith and is meaningful in the light of the Kingdom of God. If the matter is presented as a mutually exclusive choice between marrying or serving the Kingdom of God in the ministerial priesthood, a genuinely called ministerial priest will surely opt for the cause of the Kingdom of God. Nevertheless, one can question whether these are intrinsically mutually exclusive choices in the way the present discipline makes them. Nor should we be forbidden to consider the possibility of other possible ecclesiastical structures, especially in places such as Africa, where the church is searching for appropriate structures and ways of life that conform both to the gospel of Jesus and to African cultural norms.

RITUALS AND MYSTERY

African liturgies present issues of great interest not only for Africa but also for other churches around the world, not least because they stir up new momentum to understand better the core Christian mystery. Indubitably, African liturgical questions raise issues for the whole of Christian theology. Indeed, changes in rituals such as those we are discussing inevitably bring into relief issues for theological reflection and can shed new light on the mysteries of salvation, understanding of which till now has been confined to what the Greco-Roman categories have allowed.

First, one can consider the general notion of salvation. A European missionary once asked me: "Do you think that by changing the rites through your inculturation, more people will be saved? Did not your forefathers who had been baptized through the Roman rite receive forgiveness for their sins?"

I answered him: "I believe that an African who has been saved under a European mantle has not been fully saved. It is a lame salvation, a crippled salvation." It is enough just to observe current African Christian gatherings for liturgical celebration. From now on, when we celebrate, we must celebrate in our own style. We are no more in the clutch of the foreigners when we celebrate the mystery of our salvation. In this regard, the bishop of Bobo Dioulasso has said: "If God saves me, he saves me as an African and not as a European, . . . otherwise, he will make me a failure and that will not be the glory of his redemption."[5]

When we celebrate a Christian mystery with traditional African symbols, do we still celebrate the same saving mystery as the rest of the church? The answer is simultaneously both yes and no. When we translate a reality from one language to another, do we mean the same thing? Take the phrase "as white as snow" in Psalm 50. Does it mean the same thing as "as white as strands of cotton"? Yes, because in each case the referent is "whiteness." No, because cotton is both physically different from snow and—*as culturally constructed*—whiteness is not necessarily identical in different social contexts.

With the new symbols in use in Christian rites in Africa, the message at one level is the same—it is all about the new life in Christ and the salvation he mediates. Baptism celebrated with white kaolin, banana leaves, and feigning death still means new life. The physical environment and other such things (for example, where a given ritual is celebrated, the kind and location of the altar, and the words used to proclaim the event celebrated) should show that Christ is the foundation and goal of this new life. Nevertheless, there is change in emphasis, pitch, and tone that African symbols bring to the theology of baptism.

If local food and drink are used in the eucharist meal, we still proclaim Christ's death and resurrection as a redeeming act, but we put a distinct theological accent on the incarnation of the Word in the eucharist. God is a completely "other," an inexhaustible reality, but God calls humanity to join divinity—as friend, as brother, as sister—in God's own environment. To take part in an African meal in memory of Jesus, is to *reactualize* or *re-present* the life of Jesus as gift and praise to the Father through his passion and death; it is to join the concept of the Easter memorial (a reactualization of the Passover of Exodus 12) in a radical way. There successive generations enjoy liberation from the Egyptians and proclaim that God really has saved them in their own situation. To make the Lord's supper a reality today, we have suggested that today's bread and wine should be introduced in the eucharistic celebration.

When Jesus is proclaimed "King of the universe" and "Living God," it is not the same as when he is named "Leopard who doesn't fight with another for a forest." The two expressions do not concern every individual who celebrates the same Christ. Put together in an African Muntu,

King and Living God do not spiritually nurture a person. Meanwhile, calling Christ "Leopard" fills the African with respect and helps the African to better understand Christ and the encounter with Christ. In addition—because of the limits of all metaphors—no human word or expression fully explains the mystery of Christ. At the same time, these new titles spontaneously given to Jesus in numerous songs of our African liturgies have given new perspectives to African Christology, where Jesus is thought of as someone with a complex face—as elder, proto-ancestor, and liberator as well as initiator, healer, and chief.[6]

RITUALS AND EARTHLY RELATIONSHIPS

The African rituals, such as those for the consecration of religious, various seasonal blessings, and blessings for bewitched children, have introduced into Christian worship a perception of life and the world different from the bottom line of classical Christian theology. This conception is one of a world constructed as a place of participation in life coming from God as the ultimate reality and summit. This perspective is populated with ancestors and intermediaries. It has a certain two-faced aspect—one invisible and transcendental facing the visible world, but also an immanent transcendent. The world is unsafe and unstable, a zone where both dimensions meet and interact in parental lives and through ritual words, gestures, and symbols. The diversity of the signs utilized in these celebrations is the first clue of the structure of the new universe: palm wine, kola nut, white kaolin, leopard skin, banana tree, goats rope, arms, soil and seed, hairs. People who celebrate with all these things are close to nature and live in close communion with it. These elements have not been introduced haphazardly into Christian worship. Rather, they have faced scrutiny and have been found justified by authorities. The use of blood, not only as an expression but as an act of self-donation, reveals the notion of a world where there is interaction of material and spiritual elements. Recall, for instance, the blessing at the time of sowing. It is worth noting that the knotted strings of the Sacred Heart Sisters in Mbandaka are kept in a sacred place. Nor is it by chance that the white linen stained with the blood of the sisters after their pact is also reserved near the altar.

The theology that is elaborated in our communities—where there is a continuous mutual readjustment between the conception of the world and theology—is on solid ground. We no longer exclude the African and animist vision of the world from Christianity. The remote *Deus ex machina* perched on a remote summit has come down and become our partner in a new covenant. Our God is a God who establishes direct relationships with humanity, eliminating the distance between humanity and deity with almighty power, making Godself small and poor, quite contrary to the traditional conception of a far-off deity.

RITES AND RELATIONSHIPS
WITH THE TRANSCENDENT WORLD

African liturgies are not closely related to the transcendental world even when the ancestors are remembered. The invocation of the ancestors does not express a desire on our part to join them. Rather, we traditionally call on them because of our desire to save, enhance, and continue our present life on earth. The image of heaven and angels evoked in liturgical celebrations is nothing but a model for our present life. The rite of religious consecration provides us in a special way with an eschatology that is different from the one we find in classic traditional Christian rites. The classical consecration rites invoke heaven and angels to establish a relationship between the visible and the invisible in religious life. Bantu rituals are silent with regard to heaven, because for the Bantu everything takes places in the present world and the life after death is a continuation of this life. In that conception, if we have worked for the triumph of good and the victory of life over death and evil, we will continue to live beyond death and enjoy victory in the company of our ancestors. But if one has led an evil life and therefore deserves to be condemned, he or she is fated to join the eternally damned. In that position one has no relationship whatsoever with the ancestors.

The God of the Bantu does not wait for the death of humans to settle accounts. In the new rite of consecration a special stress is placed on the mutual relationship between the world of the living (the present world) and the world of the dead by invoking the ancestors. The rite also invites a special participation of the whole cosmos—in all its facets—in the liturgy that celebrates and the ongoing process that is the reality of human life on earth. All this leads to recognition of an eschatology in which exists a close interrelationship between space and time, between past and future, between the material world and the Transcendent, between the living and the ancestors, between the world of spirits, material things, and human beings.[7] Thus the religious horizon manifested in these African rites does not appear to be concerned with the future but with a reality that is in the process of growth. This growth is manifested as being in full communion with our earthly environment and with those who share it. This is why a Bantu religious sister, priest, or brother is deeply concerned with maintaining a close personal relationship with his or her ancestral social group—that is to say, with everyone with whom he or she shares life.

In the end—in the theology of salvation—the determining factor in African theology is the invocation of the ancestors. In the eucharistic prayers of Black African churches,[8] and in almost all rites of reconciliation and consecration, one finds the invocation of the ancestors. Africans associate themselves with their ancestors in all the events and undertakings of their life, and everything has a religious, even "sacramental" dimension. By invoking parents or ancestors in the very heart of Christian religious rituals, Africans proclaim that the world is a zone of participation in a parental circuit and that future participation must enable us to reinforce our communion in life with everyone. Any participation that does not strengthen communion with the ancestors is like placing a new store in a building without ensuring it of support by the foundation. In all the spiritual undertakings our relationship with the ancestors must be taken into consideration. To say the important thing once again, this relational reality is expressed especially clearly in the rites for the profession of religious and in the invocation of the ancestors during the eucharist celebration, when their presence is sought.

This invocation of ancestors has serious consequences for the theology of salvation in Jesus Christ as it has begun to be understood in Africa. For this theological reflection not only touches the structure of every family but is also integrated in the process of our final salvation. It situates different levels of communication between a Muntu and God and between Christ and the ancestors. Between these two levels there will not be any conflict, since for a Muntu the scope of communion with the ancestors was never limited to themselves. It was a necessary criterion for the growth of life. Now Christ has presented himself in this life as both the beginning and the end, that is, as the fullness of life. The ancestors find themselves still in connection with humanity in their effort to reach the fullness of life. Thus recourse to the ancestors' life is not something unnecessary and optional but the only way for Muntu Christians to be complete both in their adherence to Christ and in their aspiration to reach life in its fullness.

AFRICAN LITURGIES AND THE BIBLE

If African liturgies involve African symbols, to what extent are they still biblical? Must biblical messages necessarily entail domination of religious imagination by biblical symbols? Are the material elements found in the Bible to be preserved at all costs? Is one unfaithful to the Bible if one uses palm oil in the place of olive oil, or if on Palm Sunday one uses *buis* instead of palm leaves? In the eucharistic celebration on Sunday, what is the concrete theological consequence if one reads a passage from one's ancestor—his life or writings—in the place of or alongside the biblical readings? We raise these questions not because they concern only

Africa. Both Europe and India have raised this very same problem. Why, they ask, can't one read non-Christian texts when they are in harmony with the mystery being celebrated?

We know that there exists a strict and a fundamental relationship between the Bible and the Christian liturgy.[9] As a matter of fact, the Bible is the first liturgical book because it was the first book used for the liturgy by the early Christians, following the Jewish tradition, particularly that of the synagogue service. In that liturgy public proclamation of the word of God was paramount. The Bible is also the source, par excellence, of the memorial of the paschal mystery of Christ, which gives the basic form to the Christian liturgy in the New Testament. It must, therefore, be kept in mind that the Bible—in its own turn—is born of the liturgy to the extent that liturgy shaped the composition and elaboration of the Bible.

A change of rite and of language necessarily demands another way of interpreting the Sacred Scriptures. The translation of the Bible into African languages obliges us to use images other than those used by the biblical writers. Only this can make clear and relevant the biblical message to the people of Africa. For example, the biblical phrase "as white as snow" is often replaced by the expression "as white as a strand of cotton" in liturgical songs in some parts of tropical Africa. The Missionaries of Africa in Bukavu (Congo) have translated all the psalms of the liturgy of hours in tropical images.[10] In their book of prayer, "more white than the snow" becomes "more brilliant than the sun." Benezet Bujo has proposed that we translate John 15:1-2 ("I am the true vine . . . ") replacing "vine" with "fig" [Latin, *ficus*]. This African tree represents the ancestors and is sometimes planted on tombs.[11] A translation is always an interpretation. Since the Bible is the living word of God, its revelation is inexhaustible by human expressions or interpretations. The living word of God does not addresses itself to us independent of our concrete historical situation but in our real, social situations, where God tells us that God's ways are not our ways. Moreover, we must also overcome the idea that divine revelation is limited to Jewish-Christian writings, however important and privileged these writings are. African Bible scholars have already made a beginning reflecting on the ramifications of these insights.[12]

To the extent in which the word of God is translated to the African context, there will be an African understanding of the Bible, and this African understanding of the Bible will definitely assist our liturgical development and vice versa. This does not mean that all original biblical language and symbols must be banished from the non-Mediterranean world. In fact, a great many biblical symbols are relevant and meaningful to people of every culture. Examples of things that communicate across many cultures include the majority of the following—water, oil, bread, pearl, rock, salt, the cross, fire, light, vine, shepherd, covenant, church, way, door, dove, snake, ship, tomb, imposition of the hands. We can use them either as they stand or devise a form in which they are made meaningful for different social contexts. Let us bear in mind that the biblical symbols must be adapted and integrated with local symbols to make celebration true and relevant. Thus different images and symbols from African life participate in the ongoing saving action of Christ wherein he is really involved in people's lives and in sanctifying the African cosmos. The paschal mystery of Christ is not something from the past that we study as a historical event. It is present here and now in liturgy and the life of the community. In the proclamation of the word, God is incarnated once again, and that incarnation enriches and is enriched by Africa.

Conclusion

An African Christian liturgy has been born. And we have been examining how its most significant traits have developed. Because of the incarnation of God into humanity, Christian prayer is a mirror in which God and humanity are held up to view. God is the source, the one who inspires us to pray and who takes the initiative in the encounter. But the experience of this encounter is one marked by two subjects, not one.

In Africa the mirror of the prayer reflects the traits of African humanity. The differences from images reflected in other cultures are no disadvantage to Christianity but an enrichment. For the African experience of prayer opens new avenues of symbolic expression and can help non-Africans as well as Africans see God in new ways. To the extent that liturgical prayer responds to and reflects everyday life, it cannot remain identical in every location and in all places. Jesus Christ—the same for all—encounters each one in our particularity in a unique relationship.

Christian prayer is the work of God (the *opus Dei*, as the Benedictine tradition terms it) before it is our affair. The death and resurrection of Jesus the Christ give it power and specificity. Christian prayer in Africa must be oriented continually and fundamentally to the work of salvation accomplished by and being accomplished in the Christ. Sung and confessed with different melodies, different rhythms, different symbols, the richness of this unique Christ is nothing less than magnificent. African theological discourse introduces to prayer a special conception of the world and our life in God, insight into God and God's intermediaries on earth—the ancestors of every people.

Ancient Bantu hymnody sings new words in new melodies and helps reflect the African faces of Jesus Christ. No image, no human word exhausts the mystery of Christ. That is why one must always find new words and symbols. Christian liturgy is not a finished book whose pages one turns to find the only valid tones and words. It is history on the move, a history of love that must ceaselessly find the apt gesture, the right word, the pregnant symbol that fit the situation.

Notes

1. THE HUMAN IMPRINT ON THE LITURGY

1. L. M. Chauvet, "La théologie sacramentaire est-elle an-esthésique?," *La Maison-Dieu* 188 (1991): 19.

2. Plato, *Philebus*, 51a.

3. F. Marty, *La bénédiction de Babel, vérité et communication* (Paris: Cerf, 1990), p. 133.

4. J. Y. Hameline, "Le culte chrétien dans son espace de sensibilité," *La Maison-Dieu* 187 (1991): 7-45; L. M. Chauvet, *Les sacrements: parole de Dieu au risque du corps* (Paris: Editions Ouvrières, 1993).

5. P. De Clerck, *L'intelligence de la liturgie* (Paris: Cerf, 1995).

6. John Paul II, *Redeemer of Man (Redemptor Hominis)*, 1979, no. 14.

7. P. Smith, "Aspects de l'organisation des rites," in *La fonction symbolique: essais d'anthropologie* (Paris: Gallimard, 1979); J. Y. Hameline, "Aspects du rite," *La Maison-Dieu* 119 (1974): 101-11; and R. Pannikar, *Le mystère du culte dans l'hindouisme et le christianisme* (Paris: Cerf, 1970).

8. R. Pannikar, "Man as a Ritual Being," *Chicago Studies* 16 (1977): 10.

9. Marty, *La bénédiction de Babel, vérité et communication*, p. 122.

10. The Second Vatican Council emphasizes this; see *Constitution on the Sacred Liturgy (Sacrosanctum Concilium)*, no. 27.

11. Marty, *La bénédiction de Babel, vérité et communication*, p. 158.

12. J. A. Jungmann, *Des lois de la célébration liturgique* (Paris: Cerf, 1956).

2. BAPTISM AND CONFIRMATION

1. L. M. Chauvet, *Symbole et sacrement* (Paris, 1987).

2. C. Mubengayi Lwakale, *Initiation africaine et initiation chrétienne* (Leopoldville: C.E.P., 1966).

3. J. Fedri, "Une expérience baptismale en pays mossi," *Spiritus* 14 (1973): 87.

4. A. T. Sanon and R. Luneau, *Enraciner l'Evangile* (Paris, 1982), p. 198.

5. Ibid., p. 184.

6. See *Devenir chrétien en Afrique* (Bobo Dioulasso, 1977), pp. 151-52.

7. *L'Eglise au service de la nation zaïroise* (Acts of the 11th Plenary Assembly of the Episcopate of Zaïre) (Brussels, 1972), p. 210.

3. THE EUCHARIST

1. L. M. Chauvet and L. Motte, *L'Eucharistie, de Jésus aux chrétiens d'aujourd'hui*, p. 182.

2. J. A. Jungmann, *The Mass of the Roman Rite [Missarum Sollemnia]*, vol. 1, trans. F. A. Brunner (New York: Benziger, 1959), pp. 1-14; R. Cabie, *The Eucharist, The Church at Prayer*, vol. 2, ed. A. G. Martimort (Collegeville, Minn.: Liturgical Press, 1986).

3. The letter of Pliny the Younger to Trajan in 112 confirms this, and so does St. Justin in the *Apology*, I, 65, as does *The Apostolic Tradition* of Hippolytus.

4. Chauvet and Motte, *L'Eucharistie, de Jésus aux chrétiens d'aujourd'hui*, p. 353.

5. L. Deiss, *The Springtime of the Liturgy* (Collegeville, Minn.: Liturgical Press, 1979), pp. 15-16.

6. L. Bouyer, *Eucharist: Theology and Spirituality of the Eucharistic Prayer*, trans. C. U. Quinn (Notre Dame, Ind.: University of Notre Dame Press, 1968), pp. 310-14.

7. Boka di Mpasi, "Libération de l'expression corporelle en liturgie africaine," *Concilium* 152.2 (1980): 53-64.

8. J. G. Davies, *Liturgical Dance* (London, 1984), pp. 22-24.

9. Michaelle, *Le pèlerin danseur* (Paris: Cerf, 1978).

10. *Church of the Lord*, Book of rituals cited by P. Tovey, *Inculturation: The Eucharist in Africa*, Alcuin/GROW Liturgical Study 7 (Bramcote, Nottingham: Grove Books, 1988), p. 21.

11. P. Abega, "La liturgie Camerounaise," in *Médiations africaines du sacré*, *Cahiers des Religions Africaines* XX-XXI, 39-42 (1986-1987).

12. *Tshiondo* (tam-tam), 2 May 1989.

13. One can see this in Bimwenyi Kweshi, *Discours théologique négro-africain* (Paris, 1981), chap. 8; François Kabasele Lumbala, *Chemins de la christologie africaine* (Paris: Desclée, 1986); L. Museka Ntumba, *Nomination africaine de Jésus-Christ, Quelle christologie?* (Louvain-la-Neuve, 1988; Kananga, 1989).

14. See the preface of the celebration at Saint Merry, below; also see those one finds in *A travers le monde célébrations de l'Eucharistie* (Paris: Cerf, 1981).

15. *Pâques africaines d'aujourd'hui* (Paris: Descleé, 1989), pp. 26-28.

16. J. A. Jungmann, *Die Stellung Christi* (Munster in Westf.: Aschendorff, 1925, 1962), p. x; in English, *The Place of Christ in Liturgical Prayer* (Collegeville, Minn.: Liturgical Press, 1989).

17. See J. Deshusses, ed., *Sacramentaire Grégorien*, n. 2342; "La doctrine eucharistique dans la liturgie romaine du Haut Moyen Age," in *Signes et rites de l'Eglise occidentale du Haut Moyen-Age* (Rome, 1987), pp. 547-48.

18. The prayers that follow can be found in *A travers le monde célébrations de l'Eucharistie* (Paris: Cerf, 1981).

19. Benezet Bujo, *Christmas, God Becomes Man in Africa* (Nairobi, 1995). See also Benezet Bujo, "Nos ancêtres, ces saints inconnus," *Bulletin of African Theology* 1 (no. 2, 1979): 172-73.

20. C. M. Mulago, *La religion traditionnelle des Bantu et leur conception du monde* (Kinshasa, 1973). L. V. Thomas and R. Luneau, *Les religions d'Afrique noire* (Paris, 1981).

21. Thomas and Luneau, *Les religions d'Afrique noire*, pp. 182-83.

22. Ibid., p. 85.

23. H. Marrou, "Survivances païennes dans les rites funéraires des donatistes," in *Hommages à Joseph Bidez et à Franz Cermont* (Bruxelles, 1949), p. 197.

24. *Sermo*, 361, 6, in P.L. 39, col. 1601.

25. *De cura pro mortuis*, 18, 22.

26. Matungulu Otene, *Etre avec* (Lubumbashi: St. Paul Afrique, 1981), p. 55.

27. Bamuinyikile Mudiasa, *La mort et l'au-delà chez les Luba du Kasayi* (Lubumbashi, 1969), p. 108.

28. Nkongolo Wa Mbiye, *Le culte des esprits* (Kinshasa, 1974), p. 21.

29. René Jaouen, *L'eucharistie du mil* (Paris: Karthala, 1995).

30. Kurt Hruby, "Le geste de la fraction du pain ou les gestees eucharistiques dans la tradition juive," in *Gestes et paroles dans les diverses familles liturgiques* (Conference Saint Serge, 24ème semaine d'Etudes liturgiques, Roma, 1978), p. 128.

31. Roland De Vaux, *Les institutions de l'Ancien Testament*, vol. 2 (Paris: Cerf, 1982), pp. 300-1.

32. Ibid., pp. 383-94. The most important thing to remember is that unleavened breads are bread for an unanticipated voyage. They are made with what is at hand. Even today in the desert regions of countries, one uses corn when there is no wheat. Even in Greece, I have had cornbread made during the annual feast of bread. Bread, in other words, is made from many different cereals.

33. See Jungmann, *The Mass of the Roman Rite [Missarum Sollemnia]*, vol. 2, p. 305; R. M. Wolley, *The Bread of the Eucharist* (London: Mowbray, 1913).

34. M. Durry, *Pliny the Younger*, vol. 4, *Lettres* X, 96 (1947), p. 74.

35. D.A.C.L., vol. 5, col. 1367.

36. Alcuin, *Epistola LXIX*, in P.L. 100, col. 289.

37. R. Naz, *Code de droit canonique*, vol. 2 (1954), p. 99; Jungmann, *The Mass of the Roman Rite [Missarum Sollemnia]*, vol. 2, pp. 312-15.

38. See Jungmann, *The Mass of the Roman Rite [Missarum Sollemnia]*, vol. 1, p. 55.

39. F. Nau, "Lettres du Patriarche Jacobite Jean X," *Revue de l'Orient chrétien* 17 (1912): 146. See also *Epistola ad Dominum Gradensen*, P.G. 120, col. 777.

40. G. G. Beck, *Kirche und theologische Literatur im Byzantinschen Reich* (Munich, 1959), pp. 535ff.

41. See the Decrees of the Council of Florence, in the year 1439, Denzinger-Schönmetzer, *Enchiridion Symbolorum*, no. 1303.

42. I. E. Rahamani, *Les liturgies orientales et occidentales* (Beirut, 1929).

43. *Fontes*, n. 772, 1062, *Collection Lacensis*, II, 505.

44. B. Neunheuser, *L'eucharistie (au Moyen-Age et à l'époque moderne)* (Paris: Cerf, 1966), pp. 110-15. I find it interesting that the Protestant translation of bread and wine in our Bantu languages replaced the word *bread* with the word for the local bread and the word *wine* with the word for the local alcoholic beverage.

45. J. J. von Allmen, *Essai sur le repas du Seigneur* (1966), p. 44; in English, *The Lord's Supper* (London: Lutterworth, 1969).

46. Cited by R. Naz, *Dictionnaire de droit canonique*, vol. 2 (1954), article 111.

47. Ibid., pp. 99-100. In addition, at the present time priests who are alcoholics are permitted to celebrate the eucharist with grape juice, a non-fermented product.

48. Jungmann, *The Mass of the Roman Rite [Missarum Sollemnia]*, vol. 2, p. 318.

49. First Provincial Synod of Milan (1565), II, 5. See also, the Synod of Almeria (1595) and the Synod of Mayorca (1639), which also accepted this practice.

50. B. Boote, "Le problème de l'adaptation en liturgie," *Revue du Clergé Africain* 18 (1963): 320.

51. A. T. Sanon, "La dimension anthropologique de l'eucharistie," *Documentation catholique* 79 (1981): 722.

52. E. Uzukwu, "Food and Drink in Africa and the Christian Eucharist," *Bulletin of African Theology* 2 (no. 4, 1980): 183-84.

53. A. Vanneste, "Une eucharistie sans pain et sans vin," *Revue africaine de théologie* 6 (no. 12, 1983): 214-15.

54. See L. Museka Ntumba, *Nomination africaine de Jésus-Christ, Quelle christologie?* (Louvain-la-Nueve, 1988; Kananga, 1989).

55. L. Mpongo, "Pain et vin pour l'eucharistie en Afrique noire, le problème a-t-il été bien posé?" *Nouvelle revue théologique* 108 (no. 4, 1986): 525-26.

4. PENANCE AND RECONCILIATION

1. See François Kabasele Lumbala, "Péché, confession et réconciliation de l'Afrique," *Concilium* 210 (1987): 95-103.

2. See the record of the 1974 theological week in Kinshasa, published under the title of *Péché, pénitence en réconciliation, tradition chrétienne et culturee africaine* (Kinshasa, 1980); and the record of the Synod of Bishops of East Africa, published in *African Ecclesiastical Review* 3 (1983).

3. Among which see P. M. Gy, "La pénitence et la réconciliation," *L'Eglise en prière* (1984). See the bibliography Gy includes in his article. I was particularly inspired by the books of C. Vogel, *Le pécheur et la pénitence dans l'Eglise ancienne* and *Le pécheur et la pénitence au Moyen Age* (Paris: Cerf, 1982).

4. See the *Rituale Romanum . . . Ordo penitentiae* (Vatican Press, 1974); *Célébrer la pénitence et la réconciliation (nouveau rituel)* (Chalet-Tardy, 1978).

5. See *Acta Apostolicae Sedis* 64 (1972): 510-14; *Notitiae* 20 (1983): 549-51.

6. See B. Adoukonou, "La médecine traditionnelle et la pastorale chrétienne," *Savanes et Forêts* 2 (1979): 170.

7. For further reading, I recommend A. F. Mujinya, "Le mal et le fondement dernier de la morale chez les Bantu interlacustres," *Cahiers des Religions Africaines* III (1969); M. Hebga, "Penance and Reconciliation in African Culture," *African Ecclesiastical Review* 25 (no. 6, 1983); S. Mbonyinkebe, "Faute, péché, pénitence et réconciliation dans les traditions de quelques sociétés d'Afrique centrale," *Aspects du catholicisme au Zaïre (CERA)* (Kinshasa, 1981); Tshiamalenga Ntumba, "La philosophie de la faute dans la tradition Luba," *Péché, pénitence et réconciliation d'Afrique* (Kinshasa, 1980).

8. See F. Lufuluabo, "La conception bantoue face au christianisme," in *Personnalité africaine et Catholicisme* (Paris: Présence Africaine, 1963), p. 116.

9. *Notitiae* 264 (1988): 468.

10. Benezet Bujo, *Christmas, God Becomes Man in Africa* (Nairobi, 1995), p. 21.

11. See H. Hochegger, *Le langage des gestes rituels* (Bandundu, 1981).

12. Katende Cyovo, *Sources* (Oral Traditions of the Zone of Gandanjika), Ceeba 72 (Bandundu, 1981): 125-29. See also L. Mpoyi Mwadia Mvita, *Luendu lua baluba* ("History of the Baluba"), 2d ed. (Kananga, 1988).

13. Gy, "La pénitence et la réconciliation," p. 127.

14. See H. Edjenguele, *La puissance de l'Evangile face au paganisme Minieh des Mbo* (Yaoundé, 1966); *Croyance et Guérison* (Yaoundé, 1973); Masamba ma Mpolo, *La libération des envoûtés* (Yaoundé, 1976). See the acts of a symposium of SECAM 1975, "Who's Who in African Witchcraft?" *PMV Africa Doss.* 12 (no. 5, 1980); P. Hebga, *Sorcellerie, chimère dangereuse?* (1979); P. Hebga, *Sorcellerie et prière de délivrance* (Abidjan, 1982); E. Milingo, *The World in Between: Christian Healing and the Struggle for Spiritual Survival* (Maryknoll, N.Y.: Orbis Books, 1984); Leny Lagerwerf, *Witchcraft, Sorcery and Spirit Possession: Pastoral Responses in Africa* (Gweru: Mambo, 1987).

15. See "Inculturating the Reconciliation Experience," *Spearhead* 92 (1986): 31.

5. MARRYING IN CHRIST

1. See K. Ritzer, *Le mariage dans les Eglises chrétiennes, du Ier au Xième siècle* (Paris: Cerf, 1970); J. Gaudemet, *Sociétés et mariage* (Strasbourg, 1980); A. Nocent, "Contribution à l'étude du rituel du mariage," *Eulogia, Studia Anselmiana* 68 (1979); K. Stevenson, *Nuptual Blessing, A Study of Christian Marriage Rites* (London, 1982); Daremberg and Saligio, *Dictionnaire des Antiquités gréco-romanes*, vol. 3, 2 (Paris, 1904); *Histoire mondiale de la femme* (Paris: P.U.F., 1965).

2. *Epistle to Diogenes*, 33.

3. Ignatius of Antioch, *Letter to Polycarp, Letters* 5, 2.

4. See Tertullian, "Ad uxorem," *Corpus Christianorum collectum a monachis* 2 (Brepols, 1954), p. 1287.

5. Tertullian, "Ad uxorem," pp. 393-94.

6. The Chaldean rite clearly reveals this in the following prayer, "Heavenly spouse, whose marriage banquet endures forever, accept the union of those who adore you . . . who place their hope in you, and who are united according to the law." See A. Raes, *Le mariage, sa célébration et sa spiritualité dans les Eglises d'Orient* (Chevetogne, 1959), p. 183.

7. See K. Ritzer, *Sacramentaire de Vérone*.

8. *Acta Sanctorum*, 1 Maii 1860.

9. See J. Goar, *Eucologium sive rituale Graecorum*, 2d ed. (Venice, 1730).

10. Martene, *Ordo 11*.

11. *Rituale Romanum de anno 1614*.

12. Council of Trent, Session 24.

13. *Sacrosanctum Concilium (Constitution on the Liturgy)*, art. 77.

14. See the *Ordo celebrandi matrimonium, Praenotanda*, 12-18.

15. See P. M. Gy, "Le nouveau rituel romain du mariage," *L.M.D.* 99 (1969).

16. Vatican II, *Gaudium et Spes (Pastoral Constitution on the Church in the Modern World)*, no. 48.

17. Vatican II, *Sacrosanctum Concilium (Constititution on the Sacred Liturgy),* nos. 77-78, and *Lumen Gentium (Dogmatic Constitution on the Church),* no. 29.

18. Common traits of marriage ceremonies in Black Africa are outlined in the following: V. Mulago, "Mariage africain et mariage chrétien," *Révue du Clergé Africain* 20 (no. 6, 1965); L. Mpongo, *Pour une anthropologie chrétienne du mariage au Congo* (Kinshasa, 1968); F. Lufuluabo, *Mariage coutumier et mariage chrétien indissoluble* (Lubumbashi, 1969); D. Zahan, "Le lien matrimonial, exemples africains," *Le lien matrimonial* (Strasbourg: Cerdic, 1970).

19. L. Mpongo, "Le mariage chrétien en Afrique noire," *Orientations pastorales* 120 (1968).

20. Martens, "Le mariage coutumier," *Orientations pastorales* 109 (1966): 369; Vanden Berghe, "Contribution à la Pastorale du Mariage en Afrique," *Orientations pastorales* 119 (1968): 242; Lufuluabo, *Mariage coutumier et mariage chrétien indissoluble*; P. Begeuerie and J. R. Beraudy, "Problèmes actuels dans la pastorale du mariage," *La Maison-Dieu* 127 (1976): 19-20; R. De Haes, "Recherches africaines sur le mariage chrétien," *Combats pour un christianisme africain* (1981), p. 38.

21. Lufuluabo, *Mariage coutumier et mariage chrétien indissoluble,* pp. 91, 112-13.

22. L. Mpongo, "La liturgie du mariage dans la perspective africaine," *Revue du Clergé Africain* 24 (no. 3-4, 1971): 195.

23. Monsengwo Pasinya, *L'esprit communautaire africain* (Kinshasa: St. Paul Afrique, 1977).

24. Mukeng'a Kalond, *Rituel Luba (Ad experimentum)* (Kananga: Centre Catéchétique, 1979).

25. Note that these responses, "He is my husband" and "She is my wife," and not the alternative, "He is my fiancé" or "She is my fiancée" indicate that the traditional marriage has already taken place. According to the customs of African society, this couple is already married, not living in sin as Western church law would see the situation.

26. Kalond, *Rituel Luba,* p. 36.

27. The conclusions of this discussion were reproduced in a series entitled "Enracinement de l'Evangile dans la culture" (Centre Pastoral Cilowa, Diocese of Mbujimayi, 1983).

28. M. Legrain, *Mariage chrétien, modèle unique? Questions venues d'Afrique* (Paris: Chalet, 1978).

29. A. Duteil, *Pentecôte sur le monde* 111 (May-June 1975), p. 15.

6. CELEBRATING THE SOLACE OF THE SICK

1. A. Chavasse, *Etude sur l'onction des infirmes dans l'Eglise latine du IIIè au Xiè siècle,* vol. 1 (Lyon, 1942), pp. 79-149, 168-75.

2. *Ordo unctionis infirmorum eorumque pastoralis curae* (Vatican: Polyglot Press, 1972), no. 24.

3. As is done already in certain parishes in Kasai; in Mbujimayi this is called *disambila dya difuululuka.*

4. Kabwe is a village in the heart of Kasai, near the Luluwa River in the center of Congo.

7. PRESBYTERAL ORDINATION

1. K. Hruby, "The Concept of Ordination in the Jewish tradition," *La Maison-Dieu* 102 (1970): 30-56.

2. C. Vogel, "The Imposition of Hands in Eastern and Western Rites of Ordination," *La Maison-Dieu* 102.

3. C. Munier, ed., *Statuta Ecclesiae Antiqua, c.93-97* (Paris, 1960).

4. Matungulu Otene, *Nos voeux à la lumière de nos traditions*; François Kabasele Lumbala, *Alliances avec le Christ en Afrique* (Athens, 1987; Paris: Karthala, 1994), pp. 301-2.

5. R. Luneau, *Laisse aller mon peuple* (Paris, 1987), pp. 160-61.

6. See *The Ritual (ad experimentum) of the Diocese of Mbujimayi, Difila bimanyinu bya lupandu ne bisambukilu* (Kinshasa: St. Paul Afrique, 1996).

8. BLESSINGS AND CONSECRATIONS

1. Mircea Eliade, *The Sacred and the Profane: The Nature of Religion* (New York: Harper Torchbooks, 1957).

2. P.L. 159, col. 1002.

3. See H. Cazelles, "Consécration du Christ et consécration de l'homme," *Cahiers marials* 86 (1973): 5-6; P. M. Gy, "Le vocabulaire liturgique latin du M.A.," *Colloques internationaux C.N.R.S.*, p. 589; M. D. Chenu, "Les laïcs et la consecratio mundi," *L'Eglise de Vatican II*, pp. 1037-49; François Kabasele Lumbala, *Alliances avec le Christ en Afrique* (Athens, 1987; Paris: Karthala, 1994), pp. 163-76.

4. See C. M. Mulago, *La religion traditionnelle des Bantu et leur conception du monde* (Kinshasa, 1973); Bimwenyi Kweshi, *Discours théologique négro-africain* (Paris, 1981); and L. V. Thomas and R. Luneau, *Les religions d'Afrique noire* (Paris, 1981) for details.

5. See E. M'veng, "Essai d'anthropologie négro-africaine," *Bulletin de Théologie Africaine* 1 (no. 2, 1979): 229-39.

6. See Kabasele Lumbala, *Alliances avec le Christ en Afrique.*

7. Englebert M'veng was murdered in 1995. It is difficult to overestimate his contributions. He was one of the greatest researchers on matters concerning African cultures and Christianity and one of the most important founders of African theology.

8. This congregation has changed its name to Servants of Bethany, and because of certain problems, the rite has been modified.

9. We have discussed sorcery, witchcraft, and rituals of reconciliation for sorcerers in relation to the sacrament of penance and reconciliation in Africa (see chapter 4, above).

9. WHAT SOCIETY? WHICH CHURCH? WHOSE THEOLOGY?

1. Ntumba M. Muanza, "Bouleversement des discours et des pratique," *Tshiondo* 2 (1989): 16; see also his article about the Tshikapa pastoral experience in *African Review of Mission Sciences* 3 (1995): 39-43.

2. See the last chapter of the book by L. Museka Ntumba, *Nomination africaine de Jésus-Christ, Quelle christologie?* (Louvain-la-Neuve, 1988; Kananga, 1989).

3. One can find more details in François Kabasele Lumbala, *Alliances avec le Christ en Afrique* (Athens, 1987; Paris: Karthala, 1994), pp. 287-94.

4. See ibid., p. 302.

5. See A. T. Sanon, "L'africanisation de la liturgie," *La Maison-Dieu* 123 (1975): 117.

6. See *Chemins de la christologie africaine* (Paris: Desclée, 1986); several essays from this book, as well as others, were published in Robert J. Schreiter, ed., *Faces of Jesus in Africa*, Faith and Cultures Series (Maryknoll, N.Y.: Orbis Books, 1991). See also L. Museka Ntumba, *Nomination africaine de Jésus-Christ, Quelle christologie?*

7. See E. J. Penoukou, "Eschatologie en terre africaine," *Lumière et vie* 31 (no. 159, 1988): 79-80.

8. See *A travers le monde célébrations de l'Eucharistie* (Paris: Cerf, 1981); and François Kabasele Lumbala, article in *Der neue Messritus im Zaire* (Freiburg, 1993).

9. See Jean Danielou, *Bible et liturgie* (Paris: Cerf, 1958). See *La Maison-Dieu* 190 (1992) and *Studia Liturgica* (1992) for good bibliographies on this subject.

10. *Louange et action de grâces* (Bukavu, 1983).

11. See Benezet Bujo, *Christmas, God Becomes Man in Africa* (Nairobi, 1995).

12. An important colloquium of African Bible scholars was published under the title *Christianisme et identité africaine* (Kinshasa, 1980).

Select Bibliography

The following bibliographic references are to materials useful in the study of the inculturation of Christian liturgy in Africa. The sources are largely in French, thus making known to the English-speaking world a body of reflection perhaps insufficiently utilized in conversations on liturgical or inculturation concerns in the English-speaking world.

1. DOCUMENTS OF ROMAN AND AFRICAN CHURCH HIERARCHIES

Cheza, M., ed.
> *Les Evêques d'Afrique parlent*. Paris: Centurion, 1992.

Congregation for Divine Worship and the Discipline of the Sacraments (Vatican Curial Congregation)
> "The Roman Liturgy and Inculturation" [Fourth Instruction for the Right Application of the Conciliar Constitution on the Liturgy (nos. 37-40)]. Rome: Vatican Press, 1994; *Origins* 23 (no. 43, 14 April 1994).

Episcopal Conference of Chad
> "Il ne suffit pas d'adapter les rituels," *La Documentation Catholique* (1988): 1067-70.

Episcopal Conference of Rwanda
> "Attention à une inculturation superficielle," *Dialogue* 109 (1985): 83.

Episcopal Conference of Zaire (Congo)
> "Les Evêques du Zaïre en visite 'Ad Limina' en 1988, à propos du rite zaïrois de la messe," *La Documentation Catholique* 1965 (1988): 649-50.

———. *Présentation de la liturgie de la messe: Supplément au Missel romain pour les Diocèses du Zaïre*. Kinshasa, 1989.

John Paul II, Pope
> "Décret 'Zairensium Dioecesium,'" Prot.1520/85, *Notitiae* (263, June 1988), 457.

2. BOOKS AND ARTICLES

Miscellaneous Collections of Papers
> *Des prêtres noirs s'interrogent*. Paris: Cerf, 1957.
> *Devenir chrétien en Afrique*. Bobo Dioulasso, 1977.

Pâques africaines d'aujourd'hui. Paris: Desclée, 1989.

Der neue Messritus im Zaire. Freiburg: Herder, 1993.

Abbaye de la Pierre-qui-Vire

Une force de salut: Le sacrement de pénitence en milieu bantou. Ed. Sainte Marie de la Bouenza. Congo Brazzavile: Presse Monastique, Abbaye de la Pierre-qui-Vire, 1967.

Abega, P.

"L'expérience liturgique de Ndzon-Melen," *Telema* 4 (no. 16, 1978), 41-50.

Boka di Mpasi

"Freedom of Bodily Expression in the Liturgy," *Concilium* 132 (1980), 53-64.

Bolengo, J.

"Un sabbat ancestral," *Jeunes Eglises* (no. 14, 1963).

Bondo, J.

"Plan for an African Easter Vigil," *African Ecclesiastical Review* 5 (1963), 309-17.

Bwanga, Z.

"Le pacte de sang africain," in *Aspects du catholicisme au Zaïre.* Kinshasa: CERA, 1981.

Chima, A.

"Africanizing the Liturgy—Where Are We Twenty Years after Vatican II?" *African Ecclesiastical Review* 25 (1984).

———. "Le rite et la théologie africaine," *Panorama Inter-Eglises* (1984).

Diangenda, K. J.

Liturgical Ceremonies of the Church of Jesus Christ on Earth through the Prophet Kimbangu. Kinshasa, 1974.

Du Fonteny, R. P.

"Evolution des méthodes d'apostolat en Afrique," *Bulletin des Missions* (no. 3-4, 1952).

Dujarier, M.

"Developments of Christian Initiation in West Africa," *Concilium* 122 (1979), 57-64.

Enoko, J.

"Pour une liturgie des défunts," *Questions Pastorales* (no. 90, 1963).

Faik Nzuji, C.

"Symboles graphiques africains dans la liturgie chrétienne," in *Vie monastique et inculturation à la lumière des traditions et situations africaines.* Kinshasa, 1989.

Fedri, J.

"Une expérience baptismale en pays mossi," *Spiritus* 14 (no. 52, 1973), 84-96.

Gravrand, A.

"La prière africaine," *Studia Missionalia* 24 (1975), 45-80.

Haes, R. de

"Recherches africaines sur le mariage chrétien," in *Combats pour un christianisme africain.* Kinshasa, 1981.

———. "Analyse de quelques symboliques dans les communautés messianiques africaines," *Revue du Clergé Africain* 20-21 (nos. 39-42, 1986-87).

Hearne, B.
> "The Significance of the Zaïre Mass," *African Ecclesiastical Review* 17 (1975), 212-20.

Hebga, P.
> *Sorcellerie et prière de délivrance.* Paris: Présence Africaine, 1982.

Jaouen, R.
> *L'eucharistie du mil.* Paris: Karthala, 1995.

Kabasele Lumbala, François
> Du canon romain au rite zaïrois," *Bulletin de Théologie Africaine* 4 (1982), 213-28.

——. "A travers des rites nouveaux, un christianisme africain," *Bulletin de Théologie Africaine* 5 (no. 10, 1983).

——. "Symbolismes religieux et symboles nouveaux," in *Médiations africaines du sacré.* Kinshasa: CERA, 1986-87.

——. "L'inculturation sacramentelle au Zaïre," *Lumen Vitae* 52 (no. 1, 1987), 75-81.

——. "Pâques africaines: le triduum pascal," *Communauté et liturgie* (nos. 2-5, 1987).

——. "Sin, Confession, and Reconciliation in Africa," *Concilium* 190 (1987), 74-81.

——. *Pâques africaines d'aujourd'hui.* Paris: Desclée, 1989.

——. "Prier à l'africaine," in *Vie monastique et inculturation à la lumière des traditions et situations africaines.* Kinshasa, 1989.

——. Symboles africains et célébration liturgique," in *Théologie africaine, bilan et perspectives.* Kinshasa, 1989.

——. "Christ as Chief," in Robert J. Schreiter, ed., *Faces of Jesus in Africa.* Maryknoll, N.Y.: Orbis Books, 1991, 103-15.

——. *Symbolique bantu et symbolique chrétienne: Rencontre dans la liturgie.* Kinshasa, 1991.

——. *Alliances avec le Christ en Afrique: Inculturation des rites religieux au Zaïre.* 2d edition. Paris: Karthala, 1994.

——. *Liturgies africaines: l'enjeu culturel, ecclésial et théologique.* Kinshasa: Ed. Facultés de Théologie, 1996.

Legrain, M.
> *Mariage chrétien, modèle unique? Questions venues d'Afrique.* Paris: Chalet, 1978.

Lucas, V. W.
> *Christianity and Native Rites.* London: Central Africa House Press, 1950.

Luykx, B.
> "Culte chrétien et âme africaine," *Q.C.* (no. 88, 1963).

——. "Une liturgie de la messe pour l'Afrique," in *38ème semaine de missiologie.* Louvain, 1963.

——. *Culte chrétien en Afrique après Vatican II.* Immensee: Nouvelle Revue de Science Missionnaire Supplemente XXII, 1974.

Martin, M. L.
> "Quelques symboles et rites de l'Eglise Kimbanguiste," in *Médiations africaines du sacré.* Kinshasa: CERA, 1986-87.

Mbuyamba, L.
> "Promesses de la tradition musicale dans l'effort d'adaptation de l'Eglise du Zaïre," in *Aspects du Catholicisme au Zaïre.* Kinshasa: CERA, 1981.

————. "Le chant rituel," in *l'Afrique et ses formes de vie spirituelle*. Kinshasa: CERA, 1983.

Mpongo, L.
"La liturgie du mariage dans la perspective africaine," *Revue du Clergé Africain* 26 (nos. 3-4, 1971).

————. "Evangélisation et liturgie," *Telema* 2 (no. 3, 1976), 5-15.

————. "Le rite zaïrois de la messe, ses caractères spécifiques," *Spiritus* 19 (1978), 436-41.

————. "Contemporary African Celebrations of the Blessing of Baptismal Waters in the Roman Rite," *Concilium* 178 (1985), 62-69.

————. "Pain et vin pour l'eucharistie en Afrique noire: le problème a-t-il été bien posé?" *Nouvelle Revue Théologique* 108 (1986), 517-31.

————. "Le rite zaïrois, quelques unes de ses caractéristiques," in *Médiations africaines du sacré*. Kinshasa: CERA, 1986-87.

Mubengayi Lwakale, C.
Initiation africaine et initiation chrétienne. Leopoldville: C.E.P., 1966.

Mulago, V.
"Le pacte de sang et la communion alimentaire: pierres d'attente de la communion eucharistique," in *Des prêtres noirs s'interrogent*. Paris: Cerf, 1957.

————. "Mariage africain et mariage chrétien: Perspectives liturgico-pastorales," *Revue du Clergé Africain* 20 (1965), 547-64.

————. *Un visage africain du christianisme*. Paris: Présence Africaine, 1965.

————. "Sauver la vérité des sacrements dans nos jeunes chrétientés," *Revue du Clergé Africain* 21 (1966), 274-91.

————. "Symbolismes dans les religions traditionnelles africaines et sacramentalisme," *Revue du Clergé Africain* 27 (no. 4, 1972).

Mutembe, P.
"Christianisation de certains rites funéraires au Rwanda," *Foi et Culture* (March-April 1970).

M'veng, E.
L'art d'Afrique noire: Liturgie cosmique et langage religieux. Paris: Mame, 1964.

————. "Christ, Liturgie et Culture," *Bulletin de Théologie Africaine* 2 (no. 3, 1980).

————. "Le vêtement liturgique africain," in *Médiations africaines du sacré*. Kinshasa: CERA, 1986-87.

Nothomb, D.
"Une eucharistie sans pain et sans vin," *Euntes-Digest* 16 (1983), 429-40.

Nyamiti, Charles
"The Transformation of Tribal Initiations into the Rituals of Initiation Sacraments and Sacramentals," *Cahier des Religions Africaines* 9 (1971), 5-57.

Ouedraogo, R.
"Recherches pour un cheminement catéchumènal en pays Mossi," *Le Calao* 47 (no. 3, 1979).

Pobee, John
"The Kenosis of Christian Worship in Africa," *Studia Liturgica* 14 (no. 1, 1981), 37-52.

Rosny, E.
    "Renouveau charismatique et transe en Afrique," *Etudes* 370 (August 1989), 667-78.
Sanon, A. T.
    "L'Africanisation de la liturgie," *La Maison-Dieu* 123 (1975), 108-25.
    "La dimension anthropologique de l'eucharistie," *Documentation catholique* 78 (1981), 721-28.
Sanon, A. T., and Luneau, R.
    Enraciner l'Evangile. Paris: Cerf, 1982.
Shorter, Aylward
    "African Eucharistic Prayer," *African Ecclesiastical Review* 12 (no. 2, 1970), 143-48.
Smet, S. de
    "De Zairese liturgie," *Tijdschrift voor liturgie* 60 (1976).
Tovey, P.
    Inculturation: The Eucharist in Africa. Alcuin/GROW Liturgical Study 7. Bramcote, Nottingham: Grove Books, 1988.
Tshibangu, T.
    "Une liturgie africaine," *Eglise vivante* (no. 12, 1960).
————. "Une liturgie adaptée à l'Afrique," *Afrikakring* 2 (no. 2, 1967).
Uzukwu, E.
    "Blessing and Thanksgiving among the Igbo (Nigeria): Towards an African Eucharistic Prayer," *African Ecclesiastical Review* 15 (1973).
————. "Food and Drink in Africa and the Christian Eucharist," *Bulletin de Théologie Africaine* 2 (no. 4, 1980).
————. "Africa's Right to Be Different," *Bulletin de Théologie Africaine* 4 (no. 7, 1982), 87-109.
————. *Liturgy: Truly Christian, Truly African*. Kenya, 1982.
————. "Liturgical Celebration and Inculturation," in *Igbo Christian Communities: Twenty Years after Vatican II*, in *The Nigerian Journal of Theology* 1 (no. 2, 1986).
Van Cauwellaert, J.
    "Coutumes locales et liturgie," in *Mission et Liturgie*. Bruges: Abbaye de Saint-André, 1959.
Vanneste, A.
    "Une eucharistie sans pain et sans vin," *Revue Africaine de Théologie* 6 (no. 12, 1983), 205-18.
Weman, Henry
    African Music and the Church in Africa. Translated by Eric J. Sharpe. Acta Universitatis Upsaliensis. Uppsala: Lundequistska Bokhandeln, 1960.